Gospel
in
Action

Gospel
in
Action

A New Evangelization Day by Day

Edited by
Gary Brandl and Thomas Ess, OFM

Foreword by
Brendan Leahy

New City Press
of the Focolare
Hyde Park, New York

Published in the United States by New City Press
202 Comforter Blvd., Hyde Park, NY 12538
www.newcitypress.com
©2013 New City Press

Cover design by Leandro de Leon

Concept and chapter structure based on:
Chiara Favotti (ed.), *Una buona notizia*, (Rome: Città Nuova, 2012).

Experiences printed with permission from various issues of *Living City* magazine and the
New City Press (Hyde Park, NY) publications, Tom Masters and Amy Uelmen, *Focolare: Living
a Spirituality of Unity in the United States* (2011), Doriana Zamboni (ed.), *Glimpses of Gospel
Life* (2004), and John Olsen, CFX and Thomas Masters (eds.), *The Family and Prayer* (1991).

Library of Congress Cataloging-in-Publication Data:

Gospel in action : a new evangelization day by day / Gary Brandl and Thomas Ess (eds.) ;
foreword by Brendan Leahy.
    p. cm.
Includes bibliographical references.
    Summary: "Gospel in Action is a blend of spiritual advice from the long tradition of the
Catholic Church with modern examples of how that advice is lived out in today's world.
After each excerpt from a saint, an encyclical, or a spiritual leader, you have a story from an
ordinary person making choices day after day" "[summary]"--Provided by publisher.
    ISBN 978-1-56548-486-3 (alk. paper)
    1. Christian life--Catholic authors. 2. Catholic Church--Doctrines. I. Brandl, Gary. II. Ess,
Thomas.
    BX2350.3.G67 2013
    248.4'82--dc23
                            2012038362

Printed in the United States of America

Contents

Announcing and proclaiming is not the task of any one person or a select few, but rather a gift given to every person who answers the call to faith. Transmitting the faith is not the work of one individual only, but instead, is the responsibility of every Christian and the whole Church. (92)

This demands learning a new manner of responding ... involving not only a state of mind but personal deeds and public testimony as well as the internal life of our communities and their missionary zeal. This will not only add greater credibility to the Church's work in education and selfless dedication to the poor but also strengthen the ability of every Christian to engage in the conversation taking place in all areas of living and in the workplace, so as to communicate the gift of Christian hope.... The world must witness this manner of response, based on the logic of our faith, in not only the Church as a whole but the life of every Christian. (119-120)

Instrumentum Laboris 2012 Synod of Bishops

Foreword

The Gospel, Evangelization and Life

When I mentioned the gospel in a recent televised panel discussion, the host quipped, "What's the gospel got to do with it?" His question says a lot. It's true — many people often don't link the gospel and life. It's considered something that at best you read or study, meditate or pray. How easy to forget that it's meant for *living*. It is intended to be our very heartbeat, shaping our personal decisions and actions in society.

Focus on *living* the gospel resonates with today's culture. Professor David Walsh of the Catholic University of America demonstrates lucidly that a number of philosophers are concerned not only with intellectual, ethical and spiritual issues but also and ultimately with the question of how to *live*.[1]

It comes as no surprise, therefore, that Blessed John Paul II underlined how Christians have the responsibility "to testify how the Christian faith constitutes the only fully valid response ... to the problems and hopes that life poses to every person and society." And this will come about "if the lay faithful will know how to overcome in themselves the separation of the Gospel from life, to again take up in their daily activities in family, work and society, an integrated approach to life that is fully brought about by the inspiration and strength of the Gospel."[2]

Precisely because there is a growing split between gospel and life, gospel and culture, the Church in recent years has promoted what's called "a new evangelization," one that is new in "method,

9

expression and ardor." The 2012 Synod of Bishops in Rome, for instance, was dedicated to this very theme: "The New Evangelization for the Transmission of the Christian Faith."

This book explores elements of how evangelization "works," how the gap between gospel and life can be overcome, how the gospel can be communicated in today's world. It highlights a number of key features of the new evangelization.

Living and Communicating the Gospel

To begin, a point that might seem obvious but can be overlooked — evangelization starts with personal conversion. We can never evangelize others if we ourselves are not constantly being re-evangelized, learning the "A, B, Cs", as it were, of the gospel. This life-long process starts with the simplest of circumstances and contexts — forgiving a colleague in the office, having courage to act differently among your friends in the army, cleaning the table at home. When the gospel starts to color our lives, "how" we live begins to make a difference and those around us notice. "Why do you behave the way you do? I notice the way you smile, the way you forgive ..."

And that's when something new happens. Once our life has begun to evangelize, the time for "speaking" has come — we begin to share why we do what we do. And some of those around us begin to want to share with us what we are living — even, perhaps, as one of the experiences in this book recounts, on an internet forum.

What comes across clearly in these pages is the conviction that evangelization isn't just about interior personal conversion. Nor is it just being nice to others. The challenge the gospel puts before us is to remake the Christian fabric of society. This means offering our contribution to the world we live in. To do that, as both the Blessed John Paul II and Pope Benedict XVI have repeated, we also and always need to re-make the Christian fabric of our ecclesial community, that is, based on the gospel in all its many dimensions, to build up with one another relationships in Christ. Pastors too, as an experience from the Dominican Republic shows, are called to live this in their parish life and work.

Evangelization means establishing relationships of communion between individuals, families, groups and ministers. It is what Jesus did in his earthly life. In the incarnation, he brought on earth the culture of his heavenly homeland — love, mutual giving and receiving, fraternity — and invited us to live it and share it: "That they may all be one. As you, Father, are in me and I am in you, may they also be in us, so that the world may believe that you have sent me" (Jn 17:21). Many experiences in this book bear witness to mended, renewed and strengthened relationships both within the Church and in outreach to colleagues in the workplace, neighborhood and family.

Evangelizing Together with Jesus among Us

Then, there's a further point. If we begin to promote a culture of living the gospel *together*, something important happens — an invisible but real presence of Jesus grows among us. He promised as much: "For where two or three are gathered in my name, I am there among them" (Mt 18:20). By setting out on the adventure of the gospel not just on our own but together with others, we form small living cells of the Mystical Body of Christ that is the Church. Then the One who is evangelizing is no longer this or that person but rather God among us, "Jesus in the midst" of his disciples who sense his presence.

It is *together* with Jesus among us that we find strength. That's why we need to aim consciously at enlivening the "cells" of the Mystical Body, the Church, by helping one another, meeting to share our experiences of what the gospel has done in our lives, using all the modern means for communication at our disposal to keep in contact with one another to see how things are going.

Foreword

If we let ourselves be guided by Jesus among us, then our small community will not close in on itself. It will reach out to identify around us the problems and difficulties to be resolved, the people in need, the soulless institutions that call out for life. After all, one gospel passage reminds us: "Truly I tell you, just as you did it to one of the least ... you did it to me" (Mt 25:40). In a workplace or business or hospital, putting the gospel into practice together, we begin to see things in a new way. That explains why networks of people involved in economics and mass media, politics, art and education have begun to come up with new "best practices" that reflect the gospel. In this way too we begin to get a sense of how to "evangelize culture."

It is important to emphasize that evangelization will always involve dialogue. It is never about imposing a message. To be faithful to the gospel as the Church proposes, we need to be people of dialogue. And that means approaching others with respect and "with an attitude of profound willingness to listen."[3] After all, in the sincere exchange of beliefs and convictions we proclaim our discovery of the gospel and the gospel experiences we have lived. We do so as a gift, in honest and truthful sharing of our faith experience.

We can be grateful that the Holy Spirit has provided many new ecclesial movements and communities, which Pope Benedict XVI has declared to be "a great force for evangelization in our times and an incentive to the development of new ways of proclaiming the Gospel."[4] Many of the experiences in this book come from people involved in one of these new movements, the Focolare, which was born during the Second World War precisely from a discovery of the gospel by Chiara Lubich and her first companions. As Chiara put it, "To us the words [of the gospel] seemed to have a revolutionary power, an unknown vitality: to us they seemed the only words capable of radically changing life; and of changing the life of us Christians in our times."[5]

Jesus Crucified and Forsaken as our Model and Strength

Evangelization isn't easy. Inevitably, difficulty in relationships arises, discouragement enters in and zeal diminishes. That's why an essential feature of evangelization needs to be highlighted — the mystery of the cross. It lies behind many of the experiences recounted in these pages. Jesus didn't evangelize from "outside" the human condition or simply by speaking words. Rather, he spoke from within the very depths of his life experience in our world. He did so by serving, washing the feet of others, taking onto himself their sufferings. Indeed, he identified with the human condition even to the point of the cross, where he experienced feeling abandoned by his Father. It is always striking that in the gospels of both Matthew and Mark, the crucified Jesus utters only one statement: "My God, my God, why have you forsaken me?" (Mt 27:46; Mk 15:35). This was the culminating moment of his evangelizing mission on earth. We could say this was the moment he spoke his greatest word, the Word that summarized all his other words, when he reached the utter depths of the human condition while also remaining utterly faithful to the Father. And we know that from the depths of this darkness experienced on the cross, his self-offering, out of love, unleashed upon humanity the Spirit of Love. Through his death and resurrection the gospel began to spread to the ends of the earth.

Jesus crucified and forsaken offers us a model for evangelization. For instance, he demonstrates how to "empty" ourselves out of love. He didn't impose or dominate. In order to dialogue we need to know how to "empty" ourselves of the desire we might have to impose the gospel or gain people for our cause or be successful.

Then too, Jesus crucified and forsaken provides the strength to face every obstacle to evangelization. Recognizing him in every moment of difficulty, discouragement and lack of zeal (he has taken all of this unto himself), declaring our love for him in these moments, we find the impetus to go out again to love, to share our experience, to evangelize.

This was how Chiara Luce Badano, beatified in 2010, lived the gospel. On 7 October 1990 she succumbed to a severe and aggressive form of bone cancer. Photographs of her show a young woman dressed in clothes typical of our time — jeans, T-shirts and sneakers. We see her speaking on a mobile phone. She was into the musical group U2. Not the usual images of those considered for beatification!

The local bishop who visited her was struck by a spiritual maturity beyond her years. When her mother asked whether she talked about God to the many friends who gathered around her, Chiara replied: "No. There's no point in speaking of God, I have to give him." She gave God by living the gospel-based art of loving. In particular, in facing her illness and death she remained faithful to her profound choice to follow Jesus crucified and forsaken. She often repeated a declaration of love to him, the one she recognized as her spouse in every face of suffering: "If you want it, I want it."

But having given God through living the gospel, Chiara Luce also spoke. On the last day of her life this eighteen-year-old wanted to greet the many young people gathered outside her room. Her mother hesitated to let them in but her daughter insisted, taking off her oxygen mask in order to greet them all. She explained: "Mom, young people are the future. I can no longer run. I want to hand the torch over to them like they do at the Olympics. Young people have only one life — it's worth spending it well."

It is encouraging to see in this book experiences from young people whose youth is a true gift to the Church for the new evangelization. It is a reminder to us all that by evangelizing we too keep the Church ever young.

Brendan Leahy

1.

Genuine Gospel Life

"For the nations, hearing from our mouth the oracles of God, marvel at their excellence and worth, thereafter learning that our deeds are not worthy of the words which we speak – receiving this occasion they turn to blasphemy, saying that they are a fable and a delusion."

St. Clement of Rome[1]

"The world calls for and expects from us simplicity of life, the spirit of prayer, charity towards all, especially towards the lowly and the poor, obedience and humility, detachment and self-sacrifice. Without this mark of holiness, our word will have difficulty in touching the heart of modern man. It risks being vain and sterile."

Paul VI[2]

"Above all the Gospel must be proclaimed by witness. Take a Christian or a handful of Christians who, in the midst of

their own community, show their capacity for understanding and acceptance, their sharing of life and destiny with other people, their solidarity with the efforts of all for whatever is noble and good. Let us suppose that, in addition, they radiate in an altogether simple and unaffected way their faith in values that go beyond current values, and their hope in something that is not seen and that one would not dare to imagine. Through this wordless witness these Christians stir up irresistible questions in the hearts of those who see how they live: Why are they like this? Why do they live in this way? What or who is it that inspires them? Why are they in our midst? Such a witness is already a silent proclamation of the Good News."

Paul VI[3]

Being the First to Reconcile

"There need to be saints who are living Gospels. Preaching, speaking and acting are not enough; that is all fine and good, but putting into practice what Jesus and the apostles preached is needed before all else."

St. John Calabria[4]

I was having an especially hard day at work. After an intense and difficult morning, I stepped out of my office to find our receptionist sobbing. One of the managers had been very rude to her and embarrassed her in front of other people. Knowing that this manager has a quick temper, I decided to wait until the next day to ask for her side of the incident. She sought me out immediately, however, and in a harsh voice accused me of taking the receptionist's side and not supporting her. She stormed out threatening not to return the next day.

I found myself feeling frustrated and angry about her response to my efforts to calm the situation. Then I remembered the gospel words: "Not seven times, but, I tell you, seventy-seven times ..." (Mt 18:22). I thought about my reaction and knew that I had to forgive in order to repair the relationships that had been broken.

When the manager didn't come to work the next day, I called her to apologize for what I may have contributed to the situation and listened intently as she described the previous day's events. I offered to help resolve her concerns about the receptionist and, by the end of the conversation, she decided she would return to work.

The following day I arranged a training session for the receptionist to help her perform her job better and met with the manager to resolve some other personnel matters. By the end of the morning, she too had forgiven me and a harmonious atmosphere returned.

Maria, Massachusetts

Chapter 1

The Courage to Be Different

"*It is an error, and even a heresy, to endeavor to banish the devout life from the ranks of soldiers, from the shops of tradesmen, the courts of princes, or the households of married people.... Wheresoever we are, we may and ought to aspire to the perfect life.*"

St. Francis de Sales[6]

When I entered the military I had a fairly clear understanding of my own convictions and values, but soon discovered that I had much to learn about holding on to them and expressing them openly. Like most newly enlisted, I wanted to be part of the group, but certain lifestyle choices contradicted my beliefs and how I understood I should live a Christian life. I was in turmoil. I found I didn't have the courage to be different. I simply didn't want to be left out. One Sunday during church services I felt particularly troubled. I had been out with my "new buddies" the night before and had nearly compromised my core values. During Sunday Mass all I could do was weigh my options — let go of my convictions and just have "fun," or make a definitive choice to follow God. It wasn't easy. As I prayed I told God that if he wanted me to succeed he'd have to help me find friends who shared the same values and convictions. I received a response almost immediately when I arrived at my first overseas assignment. My roommate,

18

by chance, was a devout Catholic and invited me to be involved in parish life. His example was a first inspiration. Then later, during my final two years of military service, I met a small group of people, at a base in New Mexico, who were making a real commitment to try and live out the gospel message in their military experience. I was impressed with their sincerity and genuine efforts and struggles to put the gospel message of love into daily action. Their experiences of the gospel "lived" challenged me in ways I hadn't considered, and I found myself doing small yet courageous acts of unconditional love that I would have never done before.

Edward, New York

"*They who profess to be Christ's, shall be apparent by their deeds.... It is better to keep silence and to be than to talk and not to be.*"

St. Ignatius of Antioch[7]

The Joy of Loving

"*Make sure that you let God's grace work in your souls by accepting whatever he gives you, and giving him whatever he takes from you. True holiness consists in doing God's will with a smile.*"

Mother Teresa of Calcutta[8]

Recently I was bartending at the restaurant where I work part-time during the school year. On a particularly busy day, my boss asked me to help bus tables in the sit-down part of the restaurant. The place was packed with customers waiting to sit down, and it seemed that I couldn't clean those tables fast enough. I was growing a little frustrated with how understaffed the restaurant was, and with the fact that I was doing a job that wasn't mine to do.

Out of the corner of my eye I saw someone who had been waiting for a while sit down at a table that hadn't been cleaned. I thought, "Oh well, I didn't get to that one, but at least that's one less table for me to clean." Then it hit me: "What would be the best way to love that person in this moment?" As soon as I could, I walked over to his table and asked him if he didn't mind my wiping it down for him. He looked surprised, but smiled. As I cleaned I realized that I could do more, and so I struck up a friendly conversation with the gentleman, asking him how he was doing. He looked further surprised but I could tell he appreciated it, and we talked for about a minute.

Hours later, when I finally got off work, I decided to treat myself to a much-needed break at a local coffee shop. As I approached the cashier, a voice off to the side said, "Don't worry about charging him, I got it!" I turned my head and saw him, the man whose table I had cleaned hours before. He happened to be the manager of the place! He handed me my coffee with a smile, enjoying my expression of surprise and pleasure.

Larry, Maryland

> "*If Christians would really live according to the teachings of Christ, as found in the Bible, all of India would be Christian today.*"
>
> Mahatma Gandhi[9]

Renewing a Relationship

"It has been my experience that every time people earnestly strive to live the gospel as Jesus teaches us, everything begins to change: all aggressiveness, fear, and sadness give way to peace."

King Baudouin of Belgium[10]

When I was 13, I realized that my parents' relationship had become difficult. Naturally, I hoped they would work it out, but soon I saw my perfect world crumble. My mother was going through a deep personal crisis (which I understood only later). One day she left for good and my father had to care for us children alone. I felt betrayed and disappointed by someone whom I loved. My father would ask us to pray for her, but I couldn't bring myself to do so. I was convinced that she didn't love us anymore, and I used to hang up the phone when she would call or decline the opportunity to visit with her. Once she sent me flowers for my birthday and I gave them to a neighbor.

I went through a period of rebellion and questioned all the values that I had been taught. Many times I asked why God had let all this happen. Often I would stay out all night just to avoid facing reality.

One summer, my family was invited to a retreat. It was there that I discovered how close God is to me and how Jesus died on the cross out of love for me. In fact, I discovered him as the key person in my life. Who better than he could understand me? He too, feeling abandoned and betrayed, had asked "Why." He was waiting for me, to answer all my questions. Discovering him, Jesus crucified and forsaken, turned my whole life around. Everything took on light and meaning.

Following this experience, the relationships in my family were transformed. We children began to help my father in his new job, to do things around the house, to study and to apologize immediately for any hurt we might have caused one another. The love between us grew so much that I began to feel Jesus was inviting me to take a step towards my mother, not only to forgive her but to ask for her forgiveness. It was the last thing I felt like doing but, since I had experienced Jesus' love for me, I understood that as a consequence he wanted me to start loving her.

A few days after my decision, I met with her and we began a new relationship. Although it wasn't easy to accept my mother's choice of leaving us and forming another family, in Jesus I found the one who had chosen to love beyond all limits. At times I wanted her to understand me and my desire to have her come back, but I felt powerless. Then I realized that only Jesus could help me to love her without expecting anything. I understood how much she loved us and had suffered thinking that we didn't love her anymore. More and more our relationship has become free and more profound to the point that today I can say that I love her much more than before.

Karen, New York

> "And finally, that unexpected cry, 'Why have you forsaken me?' that allows us a glimpse into the drama lived by the God-Man.... In that 'why,' to which he received no answer, every man and woman finds an answer to his or her own cry."
>
> Chiara Lubich[11]

Taking the Initiative to Love

> "You can learn more from your children than they can learn from you. They can learn from you the world of the past, but you can learn from them the world of the future."
>
> Johann Michael Friedrich Rückert[12]

As a young person I tried to live the gospel and look beyond people's outer shells. But I felt a contradiction inside because with my family, especially my father, it was difficult to do this. Every contact with my father was frustrating. It seemed as though he didn't care about what I was doing, and when he did I felt like he didn't understand me. I thought he was a failure. The divide between us was so big that I didn't think I could ever love him.

When I started school in another town, I moved out. At first, I felt relieved. I didn't have to worry about my dad or my family problems anymore. But it was the gospel command that I love my neighbor that slowly but surely helped me change the way I saw my dad.

When I would come home from school, I started to join him while he watched his favorite TV program, even if we didn't say much to each other. Then, at some point, I asked my dad to lunch. When I arranged it over the phone, he couldn't believe I'd go so far out of my way. "You're coming down? Just for me?" he asked. At that lunch, I started to discover my father and see him in a different light. There was a depth and life in him that I had never seen before. I began to understand that this man wasn't "my enemy"; he was probably my greatest advocate and protector. He wasn't the failure that I had labeled him; he was stronger and more heroic than I had ever known. Taking the initiative to love let me understand my father better and helped me start a new relationship with him.

Evelyn, New Mexico

"*You will not find peace until broken relationships − often over something very small − are reestablished.*"

Chiara Lubich[13]

23

2.

Guided by the Word

"The words of the gospel are unique, fascinating, carefully scripted, and can be translated into life. They are light for everyone who comes into this world; they are universal. When we live them, everything changes: our relationship with God, with our neighbors, with our enemies. These words gave things their proper perspective, putting everything else in second place, including our fathers, mothers, brothers, our work ... so as to give God the first place in our hearts. That is why they carry extraordinary promises: a hundredfold in this life and eternal life as well."

Chiara Lubich[1]

"The disciples are thus drawn deep within God by being immersed in the word of God. The word of God is, so to speak, the bath which purifies them, the creative power which transforms them into God's own being. So then, how do things stand in our own lives? Are we truly pervaded by the word of God? Is that word truly the nourishment we live by, even more than bread and the things of this world? Do we really know that word? Do we love it? Are we deeply engaged with

this word to the point that it really leaves a mark on our lives and shapes our thinking?"

Benedict XVI²

"Have you noticed that if you fail to learn the alphabet and the basic rules of grammar in primary school, you remain illiterate all your life, unable to read or write despite having intelligence and will? In the same way if we do not learn to assimilate one by one the words of life that Jesus has pronounced in the gospel, even though we are 'good Christians,' we remain 'gospel illiterates,' unable to write with our lives: Christ."

Chiara Lubich³

"When listening to an explanation of the Gospel, Christians should take special care to choose one key passage as their own. Then, when returning home, let them nourish themselves during the whole of the following week with this nutritious spiritual food: the word of the Lord.... The words must be placed into action and guide our lives. It must be applied to our style, our way of living, of judging, of speaking."

Paul VI⁴

Chapter 2

"... You Did It to Me"

"A good reader [of the Sacred Scripture] is not overly concerned about understanding what he reads, but rather about putting it into practice."

St. Isidore of Seville[5]

I work in the customer service department of a Florida cell phone company. At the end of a long day I received a call from an irate customer who told me bluntly that I did not know how to do my job.

My first reaction was to tell her that what was happening in her account was her responsibility because she had not followed up in a timely manner. At that moment, however, a sentence of the gospel came to mind: "Just as you did it to one of the least … you did it to me" (Mt 25:40). I then tried to serve the lady well, first by listening attentively as she went on for a while explaining herself. By the time I finally got the chance to say something, I had already decided to speak to her as I would to Jesus. I could sense her surprise; she told me that when she calls our company, whoever answers always argues with her. She went on to apologize, recognizing that her case was not my fault, nor the company's.

As we continued our conversation, I discovered in her a beautiful person. She shared that she had cancer and was receiving chemotherapy. She was feeling terrible and scared. What started out as an aggressive phone call became a moment of God. A week later I had a chance to talk to her again, and she told me that she had kept our chat deep in her heart, and it had given her a new understanding of the value of each moment.

Javier, Florida

"Since Jesus took upon himself all that is human, every burden and every guilt of the world, for that reason there is

nothing that exists in history that has been left outside of the realm of this life of God."

Bishop Klaus Hemmerle[6]

Loving Your "Enemy"

"There is nothing of the words of God that should not be fulfilled; and all that is said there has in itself the need to be put into action."

Hilary of Poitiers[7]

I teach at the university level. Each year I must complete an assessment of my achievement in the areas of research, teaching and service for the prior year. This assessment is then reviewed by the chair of my department, who prepares a summary, including illustrative examples from the student evaluations for each class taught, and makes a salary recommendation for the next academic year.

This year, when I received my chair's summary, I was stunned to see that only negative commentaries had been included. I was particularly perplexed because my teaching evaluations had improved from the prior year. There were some very high scores in several of my classes and some very positive comments from students. My chair's summary focused on two of the classes that had lower evaluations. What made it so puzzling was that the salary recommendation was fair, but it was inconsistent with the summary.

My initial reaction was one of disbelief and hurt. I read the summary several times; then, thinking that I had perhaps overreacted, I asked my husband to read it. He confirmed my perceptions. I found myself thinking, "How will I handle the meeting with the chair to discuss his recommendations before they are forwarded to the dean?" I considered the gospel passage: "Love your enemies, do good to those who persecute you" (Lk 6:27). I began thinking of the difficulty of my chair's job — having to evaluate the performance of seventeen faculty members. I did feel persecuted, but I prayed for him, and I decided I would go to the meeting with an attitude of love and respect. If there was an opportunity to call his attention to the imbalance in his commentary, I would do so ... but only if it could be done with that right attitude. I felt at peace.

Once in his office, we discussed his recommendation and he listened carefully to my perspective, taking notes all the while. He also asked for my suggestions as to how to rewrite the summary to include the positive aspects. Imagine my surprise when I arrived at the office early the next morning and found him already there, printing his new summary so that I could read and sign it before sending it on to the dean.

Michelle, Texas

"*Think, live, be: next try to express scrupulously what you think, what you are living, and what you are.*"

Henri de Lubac[8]

The Solidarity of Love

"If we are Christians, then already before living the word, grace is present in us and consequently Christ's life ... but we remain somewhat closed-in as in a cocoon. By living the Gospel, love frees the light which then increases the love: the little creature inside begins to move until it comes out as a butterfly. The butterfly is the small Christ who begins to take his place in us and then grows more and more."

Chiara Lubich[9]

One day when we were taking a test, we had to wait in one room for a long time until the whole school finished before we could go to lunch. Obviously we were all hungry and it was hard to stay in the classroom. One student sitting behind me yelled out, "I'm hungry like an Ethiopian kid!"

One of my best friends is Ethiopian and she was sitting beside me during the testing period. She is very thin and small. I noticed that the comment really hurt her, so I felt I had to come to her defense. I said to the girl who had made the comment, "Why are you being ignorant and stupid?"

Afterwards I didn't feel proud of what I had done. Deep inside I knew that I could have handled it better.

At Mass on Sunday morning I started thinking and praying about what had happened. I heard the voice within telling me that I should apologize. I said to myself that I would, but I was going to wait until Monday when I saw my classmate. Later in the evening, however, as I went to bed I was bothered by this situation and could not fall asleep. I felt as though I had to do something right then to dismantle the barrier between us.

I got up, went on Facebook, and wrote on her wall how sorry I was for what I had said, and that I had done it only out of anger.

A few minutes later she replied, thanking me for apologizing and saying that she was also sorry and we were on good terms again.

On Monday at school I saw her and she smiled at me and complimented me on my skirt. I was happy about the decision I had made because I knew I made Jesus proud.

Hazel, Texas

"I was overwhelmed by a love for the prophets and the friends of Christ. After pondering over the things the old man had said, I realized that Christianity was the only true and worthwhile philosophy."

Justin Martyr[10]

Loving to the End

"But those who look into the perfect law, the law of liberty, and persevere, being not hearers who forget but doers who act – they will be blessed in their doing."

James 1:25

One day my cousin Jim told me that another cousin, Tony, was nearing the end of his battle with cancer. Jim asked that I pray for him because it had been years since he had been to church.

Recently, in a commentary on the gospel passage "Love is the fulfilling of the law" (Rom 13:10), I had read that "this love urges us to do all the good that our neighbors may need." I immediately promised to pray, but deep inside I felt God was asking me not only to pray but to call him. It was such a strong impulse that I put aside the fact that it had been over thirty-five years since we had seen one another or even spoken. What would I say after so long? I didn't know, but I was certain that God would give me the words.

I immediately picked up the phone. Tony was very weak. Nonetheless, when he came to the phone and heard my voice, he immediately said, "Your voice warms my heart." We spoke briefly about times past, and I assured him that he was in my prayers. I wanted him to know that God loved him with an immense love, a love capable of overcoming every obstacle. We continued a little longer, talking about these things and then it was time to let him rest. I promised that I would call back the following week. Within days, however, he died. I will never forget the gift of that last conversation with him.

Shortly after, I received a letter from his sister telling me that two days before dying Tony and his wife were able to have their marriage blessed in the church, and he was able to go to confession. "I am thinking," she concluded, "that not only the talks I had with him beforehand helped this happen, but your call may have played a significant part in the 'miracle.' " I felt such a joy at this unexpected and precious news, a joy knowing that my cousin had the grace to make his peace with God and that perhaps, in some small way, I was part of that plan of God.

Kathleen, Texas

"*Everyone who listens to these words of mine and acts on them will be like a wise man who built his house on rock. The rain fell, the floods came, and the winds blew and beat on that house. But it did not fall because it had been founded on rock.*"

Matthew 7:24-25

Chapter 2

Sharing Gospel Experiences

"Nothing in the world renders more praise to God ... than the humble and fraternal exchange of spiritual gifts ... All of us who have received graces from heaven, should make every effort to share with others the divine gifts we have received, especially the gifts that can help others along the way of perfection."

St. Lawrence Giustiniani[11]

After five years of study in Rome, I returned to the seminary of my diocese for the last phase of my preparation for ministerial priesthood. One of the things I had discovered in Rome was the importance not only of studying, but also of putting the gospel into practice. After my arrival in Korea, I began to record in my diary every evening how I had meditated upon the Word and put it into practice during that day. In so doing, I was able to grasp better how God was acting in my life, and I could also share these things with others.

Two of my companions and I had a standing appointment at the end of each day. We would read together the gospel of the following day, tell one another how we had lived during the day, and would conclude with a prayer. That time together helped me a lot. On one occasion the gospel was about Jesus looking at Jerusalem and saying: "If you, even you, had only recognized on this day the things that make for peace!" (Lk 19:42). It so happened that something had made me lose peace and it took me awhile to restore it. I had teased a seminarian in a joking way, but he did not like it and was upset. Since I could not find him, I left a note for him together with a cookie and a soda. At our evening appointment I shared my experience with the others and we rejoiced together about the outcome.

On another occasion — it was during the time of exams — the gospel spoke about Jesus curing two blind persons. That day one of my fellow seminarians shared a personal problem with me: since he did very well in his studies, many were asking him to help them and he did not want to tell them no. But he still needed time to study! This tension was bothering him a lot. I tried to listen attentively, but I did not know how to counsel him. He had just finished speaking, when it came spontaneously to me to say, "Don't think that you have to do both things. Both are things of God: studying and helping the others. Do just one, that which seems to you to be the will of God for you at that moment. It is enough to be sincere with oneself." I was the first to be surprised at my words! That seminarian went back to his room very happy.

That evening I told the others what had happened. Only then did I realize that at the beginning of our dialogue, we were like the two "blind" persons. Jesus had come among us and he was the one who made us understand and see how to live his will.

Nur, South Korea

"The great word of God surpasses all the many and persua-sive discourses of the human spirit, no less than the sun on high outshines every other splendor."
St. Gregory Nazianzen[12]

Chapter 2

Caring for the Least

"The Church is an immense force of renewal in the world, not because of her strength, but because of the force of the Gospel, in which the Holy Spirit of God breathes, the God Creator and Redeemer of the world."

Benedict XVI[13]

M y aunt had a challenging personality. Once, when the hospital chaplain introduced himself with "Hello, I'm Charles!" she responded, "Hello! I'm an atheist!" She always declared her opposition to religion with great pride. We had never got on well. Then she suddenly lost her sight and hearing; a few years later, when she was 80, she suffered a stroke. Before that I didn't know how to relate to my aunt, but the change was somehow like a ticket to a new relationship.

As a Christian, I tried to live out the words of the gospel, especially, "Just as you did it to one of the least of these ... you did it to me" (Mt 25:40). This would be the measure of my love in even something as simple as helping her to put on her socks.

My aunt had always been a forceful person and this stroke seemed to reinforce her negative traits. We would quickly have an argument, and I would feel terrible because I had added more suffering to the situation. Every time I entered her room, I made firm resolutions to start again with her and to see her with new eyes but on my own I could not keep this up. So I rang one of my Christian friends to share what had happened and together it became clear that it was not my aunt who was the more forceful character and had to change, but I! I had to look beyond the physical weaknesses and disabilities and respect her as a human being with her own dignity and her own right to make choices, just as I would want to be treated if I were in that position.

Caring for her physical needs was time-consuming but just as important was caring for her soul, without ever talking about God. This also meant caring for my own soul by maintaining my prayer life and relationships with my other Christian friends, so that I could have more love to give. I decided to get some help for cleaning so that we could have time together to chat, to share, to listen to the wisdom gained from the experience of her years, to laugh together — it was so important for both of us.

A year or so before she died, my aunt began to change, letting go of the hostile attitude that she had maintained for over thirty years. Out of the blue she invited for a visit a person she had never liked very much. They had a long chat and afterwards her visitor told me that for the first time she felt there was a real relationship. She was struck by the deep expression in my aunt's eyes and felt that she was very close to God.

Shortly before dying at age 89, my aunt announced: "I think I'm not an atheist after all. Thank you for all you have done for me. You couldn't have done more."

Donna, England

"*For as the rain and the snow come down from heaven, and do not return there until they have watered the earth ... so shall my word be that goes out from my mouth; it shall not return to me empty, but it shall accomplish that which I purpose, and succeed in the thing for which I sent it.*"

Isaiah 55:10-11

3.

Rooted in Christ

"The world which, paradoxically, despite innumerable signs of the denial of God, is nevertheless searching for Him in unexpected ways and painfully experiencing the need of Him – the world is calling for evangelizers to speak to it of a God whom the evangelists themselves should know and be familiar with as if they could see the invisible."

Paul VI[1]

"Discipleship to be transparent and to be effective proclamation has to be rooted constantly and firmly in Christ himself through prayer and contemplation, through sacramental encounter with Christ in the Church. We have to be more than professional evangelizers. We need to be men and women of God-experience, living icons of Christ's love for people. We need to be utterly open to his Spirit who will lead us to communion with him. The contemplative quality of the Christian disciple-messenger resonates deeply with other Asians whose religious traditions are suffused with deep interiority."

Federation of Asian Bishops' Conferences[2]

"Indeed we cannot forget that the first task will always be to make ourselves docile to the freely given action of the Spirit of the Risen One who accompanies all who are heralds of the Gospel and opens the hearts of those who listen. To proclaim fruitfully the Word of the Gospel one is first asked to have a profound experience of God."

Benedict XVI[3]

"Anyone ... can become a source from which rivers of living water flow (cf. Jn 7:37-38). Yet to become such a source, one must constantly drink anew from the original source, which is Jesus Christ, from whose pierced heart flows the love of God (cf. Jn 19:34)."

Benedict XVI[4]

"The world does not receive the proclamation of Christ from the Eucharist so much as through the life of Christians nourished on the Eucharist and on the Word. Preaching the gospel with their lives and with their voices, they render Christ present in the midst of people. If it is united to Jesus in the Eucharist, the Christian community can and must do what Jesus has done: give its life for the world."

Chiara Lubich[5]

Chapter 3

New Life in the Workplace

"Here is the first rule of action: entrust yourself to God as if the success of things depended completely on you and not at all on God; but then put all your effort into it, as though God alone was doing everything and you nothing."

Remi de Maindreville, S.J[6]

I work in a medical center as a clinical social worker. The staff there share a great sense of collaboration, collegiality and a sincere desire to work as a team. In spite of that, they do not always agree about how to deal with particular problems. For example, most of the staff with whom I work support and encourage a woman's decision to abort a pregnancy. My view is that each life is a gift from God, and so I am troubled about the idea of encouraging anyone to have an abortion.

At the beginning of my work experience, I began to wonder whether I should stay at this job or not. At that moment I was one of three case managers in the clinic. I realized that if I remained, at least a third of the women might have an opportunity to meet someone who would not only listen to their pain, but also inform them of other alternatives and help them to overcome the obstacles to a decision in favor of life. So I decided to stay, even if it meant working amid tension with my colleagues.

One day I was walking along the hallway when a young lady ran up behind me. "Do you remember me?" she asked, smiling. I did. "How are you?" She answered with tears in her eyes: "Four years ago, I came to see you and I felt very ambivalent about keeping my pregnancy. Your respect, your words and your conviction about the value of life helped me decide to keep my baby. I now have a beautiful four-year-old daughter who has filled my life with joy. I can't imagine what life would be without her. Thank you."

Nicole, New York

38

"If a brother or sister is naked and lacks daily food, and one of you says to them, 'Go in peace; keep warm and eat your fill,' and yet you do not supply their bodily needs, what is the good of that?"

James 2:15-16

The Source of Love and Strength

"The Eucharist is life for the individual person and for society, as the sun is for their bodies and for the whole world."

St. Peter Julian Eymard[7]

While in college, I needed to maintain a full work schedule and take classes in the evening. Since I had discovered the value of the Eucharist as nourishment for my soul and as an occasion to be in direct contact with God, I wanted to attend Mass every day. Happily, there was enough time to go to Mass and get to the campus before the classes started. I would walk from my job to the church and from the church to the classroom building.

After a few weeks, the time became shorter and shorter; the work load increased and I had so little time to accomplish it. Every minute was precious, and I was getting tired, too. Sometimes I wondered, "Should I go to Mass today? Maybe I should stay in the library and study." But then I would ask myself, "What is more important in your life? Who do you love the most? Who will give you the strength to go ahead and keep loving, even when you don't feel like it?"

The gospel sentence came to mind: "Do not work for food that perishes but for the food that endures for eternal life" (Jn 6:27). Another voice would tell me, "Well, you have to study; you have to learn more and more; and it is so exciting."

But I knew what was best. I never regretted setting aside time for Mass — first of all, because I felt more love in my heart, and secondly, because somehow God always gave me enough time to do what I really had to do.

College was hard because I even had to face ridicule about my faith, about choosing moral values and making moral choices. I truly felt that it was Jesus in the Eucharist who gave me the peace and perseverance to go ahead.

Silvia, Texas

"*Where God is made great, men and women are not made small: there too men and women become great and the world is filled with light.*"

Benedict XVI[8]

Loving as Jesus Did

"*You shall be holy, for I am holy.*"

1 Peter 1:16

A boy in my class in school was making fun of me. My friends said he was mean, and they began to say bad things about him. I decided to be the one to love and to forgive him for saying things about me. I complimented him on the things he was good at, and he stopped making fun of me and everyone else, too! When he changed, my friends thought better of him. I think this is the way Jesus wants me to love!

Keri, Indiana

Renewed by the Sacraments

"The sacraments ... especially the most holy Eucharist, communicate and nourish that charity which is the soul of the entire apostolate."

Second Vatican Council[9]

Tony: Our twenty-fifth wedding anniversary was coming up.... While making plans, we thought of a couple we had met on our honeymoon who were married the same day and hour as we were. We hadn't seen them for fourteen years. We looked them up, and asked if they were interested in renewing their marriage vows with us and sharing in the celebration. They had made no special plans for their anniversary, and were delighted to accept our invitation.

Christine: When I called to tell them that our plans included a Catholic Mass, there was a moment of silence on the other end. They explained to me that they and their five daughters had been away from the Catholic Church for many years. I understood that the moment of the Eucharist would be difficult for all of them. What could be done? I bravely suggested that they go to confession with us, but the silence grew deeper and we said goodbye. Two days later the husband called to thank me for suggesting confession; they had all gone and were full of joy. They said that they were looking forward to the anniversary festivities, including the Mass.

This was just the beginning of a series of small but real miracles that the grace of God brought about through our anniversary. Others followed. For example, a friend of ours told us that while we were renewing our vows he understood that God was present in our marriage, and realized in that moment that God was missing from his life. After twelve years he returned to church and has been faithful ever since. A couple we had not seen in some years couldn't believe the change in us. When they realized that we place God first in our life, after twenty years of being far away they felt the desire to come back to him. Many of our neighbors are Catholic but had not been active in the faith. Later they told us that they had returned to the sacraments in order to participate fully in the celebration of the Mass. The most beautiful gift for us that day was that our own four sons did the same.

Tony: The priest who celebrated the Eucharist met quite a few of our friends, many of whom afterwards made appointments to see him. He told us that he felt that his sacrament of priesthood had been renewed by the love that our sacrament was giving to others in a marriage that had become a channel for the love of God to many.

Tony and Christine, New York

"You cannot light up a space – even if electricity is available –until the current's two poles are brought together."

"The life of God in us is similar. It must circulate in order to radiate outside of us and give witness to Christ, the One who links heaven to earth,and people with one another."

Chiara Lubich[10]

42

Planning Together

"Loving is forgiving, being reconciled. And reconciling is always a springtime for the soul."

Brother Roger Schütz[11]

One year I made a special effort to reach out to local priests as we prepared for Christmas. At a meeting, I proposed that we plan the Advent penitential services together. One other priest and I visited each parish to present the project. We prepared the confession stations with particular care: a small table with a Bible, and a lighted candle to honor Jesus' presence in the priest. Readers and the choir were drawn into this atmosphere of unity.

Later I saw how those who attended the service renewed their love for the sacrament of reconciliation, and felt they were in a safe place where they could open their souls to Jesus in the priest. The parish secretary told me that when she came into the church that day she sensed a special atmosphere. I was struck, too, on seeing that the priests remained for a while even after all the penitents had left the church.

Fr. Igor, Canada

"Here the Good Shepherd, through the presence and voice of the priest, approaches each man and woman, entering into a personal dialogue which involves listening, counsel, comfort and forgiveness. The love of God is such that it can focus upon each individual without overlooking the rest."

John Paul II[12]

4.

The Courage to Speak Up

"Like Christ during the time of His preaching, like the Twelve on the morning of Pentecost, the Church too sees before her an immense multitude of people who need the Gospel and have a right to it, for God 'wants everyone to be saved and reach full knowledge of the truth' (1 Tim 2:4)."

Paul VI[1]

"Those who have come into genuine contact with Christ cannot keep him for themselves, they must proclaim him. A new apostolic outreach is needed, which will be lived as the everyday commitment of Christian communities and groups. This should be done, however with the respect due to the different paths of different people and with sensitivity to the diversity of cultures in which the Christian message must be planted."

John Paul II[2]

"All of us recognize how much the light of Christ needs to illumine every area of human life: the family, schools, culture,

work, leisure and the other aspects of social life. It is not a matter of preaching a word of consolation, but rather a word which disrupts, which calls to conversion and which opens the way to an encounter with the one through whom a new humanity flowers."

Benedict XVI[3]

"There is a dynamic continuity between the proclamation of the first disciples and ours. Throughout the centuries, the Church has never ceased to proclaim the salvific mystery of the death and Resurrection of Jesus Christ, but today that same message needs renewed vigor to convince contemporary man, who is often distracted and insensitive."

Benedict XVI[4]

"To which neighbors should we open our heart, and how, having loved them? To everyone, everyone: even if it cannot always be spoken with the lips, it can be spoken with the heart ... so they notice that they are important to us, that we have considerable interest in them, that a bond is already made with them, be it only one of silence, respect. Words without sound, perhaps a smile, as can be imagined, cannot but open hearts. And as soon as that opening appears in anyone, there is no need to wait; one should speak, should say even a few words ... but speak, announce the Gospel."

Chiara Lubich[5]

Chapter 4

Facing Peer Pressure

"Here lies the test of truth, the touchstone of evangelization: it is unthinkable that a person should accept the Word and give himself to the kingdom without becoming a person who bears witness to it and proclaims it in his turn."

Paul VI[6]

S ome time ago I went with a couple of my friends to another friend's birthday party. We were having fun, listening to music and socializing.

After some time, as I was passing by one area of the house, I noticed that some girls I knew were playing a drinking game with a group of guys. This game was taking place around a table, with guys on one side and girls on the other. The objective was to down a cup of whatever drink one had, as fast as possible.

Taking obvious advantage of the girls, the guys had made up a rule that the losing team had to take off their t-shirts. Having lost the first round that's what the girls started doing.

I could see in the girls' eyes that they weren't comfortable and that they were pressured by the boys. I felt I had to stop the game and asked, "Why are you doing this? Don't you have any respect for yourselves?" They suddenly put their t-shirts back on. They were embarrassed and apologized to me. I told them they didn't need to, but to stop and think of what they were doing.

The boys' reaction was total silence as they looked at each other. They were confused since they didn't expect to see a guy step in to stop the game. I didn't worry about what others would think of me, because I wanted to live the gospel and I didn't want anyone to get hurt. The girls thanked me for caring about them.

Ron, Ontario

"It does not matter that you have no courage, provided you act as if you had courage."

St. Therese of Lisieux[7]

46

Respect in the Operating Room

"Don't ever let anyone pull you so low as to hate them."

Martin Luther King, Jr.[8]

I work as a surgical nurse in a Massachusetts hospital. It bothered me that several of my co-workers often used foul language, even in referring to the patients under anesthesia. I felt that it created an atmosphere of disrespect for the patients and for each other.

At first, I was a bit hesitant, but somehow I got the courage to tell them how I felt. In order to emphasize the point, in a kind of lighthearted way, I told them that every time they used such language, they would have to pay one dollar..

So that is what they did! I saw how it really made them more aware of how they were speaking. I used the collected money to buy cakes for different occasions, in order to strengthen our relationships in other ways.

I am happy to say that we don't have a lot of money for cakes anymore, and there is a much more respectful environment in the operating room.

Yvonne, Massachusetts

Chapter 4

Logging On to Love

"Do to others as you would have them do to you."

Luke 6:31

I belong to a provincial government employee union. Recently, our employer and the union reopened a ten-year-old grievance in hopes of finding mutual agreement. Many of my colleagues were interested in reading and writing opinions about the case on our intranet forum. Logging on one day, to my surprise I found that the union members and employer were insulting and verbally attacking each other.

My first reaction was to quit the forum, but I couldn't stop feeling sad for all the victims. I was reminded of the sentence from the gospel, "He has done everything well; he even makes the deaf to hear and the mute to speak" (Mk 7:37). I understood that I had to speak out and improve relationships in my work circle.

The next day, I sent a message encouraging dignified debate. "Writings full of hate are unacceptable in the forum," I argued. "I admire those who represent us and give their time, energy and reputation to serve us. Having the right to talk comes with the obligation to respect ourselves and others."

Reactions came quickly. Some colleagues came to see me, while others phoned or wrote, "It had to stop, thanks for your intervention!" and "You expressed the feelings that many of us were afraid to acknowledge." Virtual exchanges continued, but in a much more civilized manner.

Bernard, Quebec

"When you are called from your prayers or the Eucharistic celebration to serve the poor, you lose nothing, since to serve the poor is to go to God."

St. Vincent de Paul[9]

Facing Gossip

"Young persons ... should become the first to carry on the apostolate directly to other young persons."

Second Vatican Council[10]

Lately, when my friends gossip, I've been trying to say something nice about the person as well, or change the subject, or offer a different point of view. It was good, and I felt like I was really being a true Christian. But one time when I had tried to stop my friends from gossiping, one girl got into an argument with me. She told me that she was talking about the things that interested her. Gossip was what she wanted to talk about and I had no right to tell her what or what not to talk about. That was hard. I felt really discouraged, and I wondered whether I would ever be able to make them understand that what they are doing is not love. But then I understood that this is what it means to go against the current. There will always be opposition. I just need to stay strong and keep on loving as Jesus did.

Regina, Maryland

Chapter 4

Overcoming Evil

"On the one hand, the word must communicate everything that the Lord himself has told us. On the other hand, it is indispensable, through witness, to make this word credible."

Benedict XVI[11]

I am an elementary school teacher and am often sent to teach in the mountain villages. In those remote and hard to reach areas live terrorist groups of the extreme left, who declare themselves to be liberators of the people. I had run into them before, but I escaped by finding a hiding place among the rocks.

One day, unfortunately, I wasn't able to hide quickly enough. The terrorists kidnapped me and brought me to their camp.

During those endless days I had to undergo long periods of interrogation. Despite my fear, I tried to respond very respectfully and always tell the truth. For hours, one of them in particular tried to indoctrinate me, trying to persuade me to join their cause. When he asked for my opinion, at first I did not dare to comment. The following day, however, as he repeated his discourse, I objected. I told him that if we want to transform the structures of power that seem so unjust to us, what is needed is that we first change ourselves. While forcing myself to smile, I tried to explain to him: "This 'changing of ourselves' is the love that each one of us has for the other person."

Perhaps my words touched him; perhaps my words reminded him of principles in which he had believed. The fact is that after this interrogation he allowed me to leave. From that day on I continued to pray for him and his companions.

Recently, to my great surprise, I recognized him on television when a news account told of a terrorist who had turned in his arms to the military, and who was leaving his group.

Nelda, Philippines

"We need to witness boldly and clearly but not with anger and fear; we need to show that we believe what we say about the Lordship of the Risen Christ and his faithfulness to the world he came to redeem."

Archbishop Rowan Williams[12]

Helping the Needy

"Never, 'for the sake of peace and quiet,' deny your own experience or convictions."

Dag Hammarskjöld[13]

B*etty:* I work with a woman I'll call Grace, whose two grown children were soon to be moving out of the house. Being divorced, she realized that she would be lonely, and therefore she decided to adopt a baby. One day I overheard her saying that she had found a baby girl. When I asked her about it, she said she had found the baby through a friend after she had "put out the word." I learned that the baby was living at a crack house, along with her mother and two brothers. When Grace went to get the baby, the mother agreed, but not without leaving her two boys with Grace as well. I felt uncomfortable with what was going on, and I realized that this situation couldn't pass by without me trying to care for everyone involved as Jesus had cared for and loved me.

Frank came home and explained what was happening. One of our major concerns was Grace's second thoughts about the boys. Because they were older and harder to handle, she wanted to return them to their mother. This would have put them right back into an atmosphere of drugs and neglect. The other main concern was that Grace was keeping this baby without a legal adoption. Our first thought was to do something by which Grace would feel our concern and love. We knew that when she picked the children up, the baby was wearing only a diaper and the boys had only a pair of shorts each. So, together with our children, we went through their outgrown clothing, choosing the nicer things, folding them carefully, trying to keep in mind that we were doing this for Jesus in those children.

Frank: The next day I took the clothes to Grace. She was very happy and told me that they were exactly what she would have bought for the children if she only could have afforded it. We began to talk, and she was confused about what to do next. She knew it wasn't right to put the boys back in that house. When I suggested calling child welfare, she immediately refused because she knew that such an action would mean giving up the baby as well. She also feared that if the mother lost her government assistance she might retaliate against her. At the end of our conversation, which took place on a Friday, Grace had decided to keep the boys. She was still confused about how to handle the three kids, but knowing that I shared her concern she seemed more at peace. I suggested thinking about everything over the weekend, and then talking it over again on Monday.

That weekend, our whole family's thoughts and prayers were with Grace and the children. On Monday I wanted to look for Grace; instead she came to me smiling. Over the weekend, she had searched for and found the children's grandmother. The grandmother knew of her daughter's difficulty with drugs, but did not know where to find her. She had been worried about the children and was relieved to know that they were doing fine. She told Grace that she wanted to take the children but that Grace would be welcome to see them anytime.

From time to time Grace still brings me news of the situation. The baby has medical problems and Grace helps the grandmother by taking her to the doctor and even assisting financially when she can. The mother of the children has also contacted Grace, thanking her for what she is doing. She told Grace that some day she would like to take the children back and care for them.

Betty and Frank, Illinois

> *"If we wait for conditions to be 'favorable' before preaching the Gospel, we shall wait, every one of us, till our last day – and indeed till the Last Day."*
>
> Henri de Lubac[14]

5.

Trustworthy Witness

"Even the finest witness will prove ineffective in the long run if it is not explained, justified – what Peter called always having 'your answer ready for people who ask you the reason for the hope that you all have' (1 Pt 3:15) – and made explicit by a clear and unequivocal proclamation of the Lord Jesus."

"The Good News proclaimed by the witness of life sooner or later has to be proclaimed by the word of life. There is no true evangelization if the name, the teaching, the life, the promises, the kingdom and the mystery of Jesus of Nazareth, the Son of God are not proclaimed."

Paul VI[1]

"We wish to point out, above all today, that neither respect and esteem for these religions nor the complexity of the questions raised is an invitation to the Church to withhold from these non-Christians the proclamation of Jesus Christ. On the contrary the Church holds that these multitudes have the right to know the riches of the mystery of Christ (cf. Eph 3:8) – riches in which we believe that the whole of human-

ity can find, in unsuspected fullness, everything that it is gropingly searching for."

Paul VI[2]

"The Second Vatican Council recalled that 'The groups among whom the Church operates are utterly changed so that an entirely new situation arises.' The farsighted Fathers of the Council saw the cultural changes that were on the horizon and which today are easily verifiable. It is precisely these changes which have created unexpected conditions for believers and require special attention in proclaiming the Gospel, for giving an account of our faith in situations which are different from the past."

Benedict XVI[3]

"For our witness to be credible, as we respond to each of these areas requiring the new evangelization, we must know how to speak in ways that are intelligible to our times and proclaim, inside these areas, the reasons for our hope which bolsters our witness (cf. 1 Pt 3:15). Such a task is not accomplished without effort, but requires attentiveness, education and concern ... [we] need to devise the forms and means for speaking about God, which can then equip them to respond to the anxieties and expectations of people today, showing them how the newness of Christ is the gift which all of us

await and for which each of us yearns as the unexpressed desire in our search for meaning and our thirst for the truth."

Lineamenta for the 2012 Synod of Bishops[4]

"God put the Gospel in our hands; he gave us a new light on the Gospel, a way of seeing and understanding the Gospel fit for these times. Our first task is that of giving this Gospel to others, announcing it, spreading it. 'Woe to me if I do not evangelize' (cf. 1 Cor 9:16 said St. Paul, because he was an apostle). We – little apostles – should repeat: 'Woe to us if we do not evangelize.' "

Chiara Lubich[5]

The Choices in Life

"It is necessary that our words be roused up by the Spirit so that He gives them wings, inspiration, strength, incisiveness, beauty. Then they will be able to touch, convert, move, arouse, inflame, convert hearts, enlighten minds, awaken new energy, reveal horizons."

Fr. Piero Coda[6]

When people see the choices I am making in my life, I get both positive and negative reactions. I think that depends on whether they feel threatened, because it can be frightening to be challenged to work through your own values. For a while I focused more on living and giving an example. But lately I feel that I need to become more verbal. For example, when a conversation is taking a turn that I disagree with, sometimes on topics regarding sexuality, I have started to interject something about what I think. Sometimes it makes someone uncomfortable, and I get labeled as a goody-goody.

Other times I encounter respect. Recently I was walking to the train with a colleague and just out of the blue she looked at me and said, "You are a Christian, aren't you?" I felt like she was trying to put together the pieces of what she saw in various interactions. So this started a long conversation where I mostly just listened, trying to give space for her to share what was in her soul, because she is really searching.

Elizabeth, Massachusetts

"In your hearts sanctify Christ as Lord. Always be ready to make your defense to anyone who demands from you an accounting for the hope that is in you; yet do it with gentleness and reverence."

1 Peter 3:15-16

Chapter 5

Trusting in Providence

"Do not inscribe in the plan of your life a deformed, impoverished and falsified content.... If necessary, be resolved to go against the current of popular opinion and propaganda slogans!"

John Paul II[7]

am: I was approaching twenty-one years of employment with the same company, making a good salary, and receiving good benefits. I felt secure in spite of rumors that our department was going to close, but last summer that was exactly what happened. All the staff of our department were assigned to a placement center for sixty days.

During the first few days, I had an interview within the company. The interview went well, but as I walked out the door, a little voice from inside kept saying, "What that department is involved in is unacceptable to your beliefs." This reaction caught me completely by surprise, for I had worked in the very same division twenty-one years before and thought nothing of it. But I had since made the choice to put God in the first place in my life, and I couldn't turn my back on him now.

I talked it over with my wife, Rita, and we agreed that I should not take this particular job. The next day I turned down the offer that would have given me the same pay, benefits and security to which we had become accustomed. As we watched twenty years of hard work and dreams — all our security — vanish before our eyes, the whole family turned to God.

Rita: When Sam and I sat down to discuss the job offer, the idea of holding on to the security was tempting, but we really had the feeling that God was asking us to say yes to him by turning our backs on material worries and really placing ourselves in his hands, trusting in his providence.

Sam and Rita, Missouri

Returning Good for Evil

"If one person, with his or her word gives birth in the soul of a neighbor to love for the Lord, this in a way produces the Lord, because it gives birth in the heart of the one who hears that word, and the one who speaks becomes mother of the Lord."

St. Gregory the Great[8]

I was walking along the road in Manila. A youth approached me and when a short distance away unsheathed a knife and pointed it at me. "Give me all your money!" he demanded. "Certainly," I replied, "and I think that you are hungry too. Look, there's a restaurant here, come and eat and drink what you want." He was taken aback a little, but he followed me. He ate and drank until he'd had enough and I asked with love about his family. He told me he needed everything: food, clothes, shoes ... I promised him that the next day I'd prepare a box of clothing for him and I gave him my address. He left in better spirits.

The next day he arrived, hesitant, ready to run, fearing a trap. He took the parcel and said to me, "My neighbor is as poor as me and needs some help." I invited him to return the next day to collect some things for his friend. When he did come back, I smiled at him and offered him the new parcel. I was happy because I was giving food and clothing to Jesus in him. He threw himself on to his knees and shaking, exclaimed, "You are a priest, listen to my confession." I listened and he left happy. From that time, he, his family and his friend's family come to our community meetings.

Fr. Gerald, Philippines

"We can accompany Our Lord, without any trouble of our own, merely allowing ourselves to be carried by Him, according to the divine good-pleasure, as an infant in the arms of its mother."

St. Francis de Sales[9]

Chapter 5

Love Speaks Louder than Words

"We are in an age in which ... the one gospel has to be proclaimed both in its great, enduring rationality and in its power that transcends rationality, so that it can reenter our thinking and understanding in a new way."

Benedict XVI[10]

Taking a course in international contemporary literature, I was excited to be learning about people from other countries. I tried to love my classmates and my professor by listening well and participating in class discussions. Things were going fine until we were assigned our third book. It began with vulgar language and scenes, and I knew right away that I couldn't continue reading it. The other students agreed with me but felt they "just had to get through it."

I shared this struggle with some of my friends who also want to put the gospel into practice in daily life, and we agreed that I should share my concerns with my professor. The next day I went to him with my problem. He reassured me that the book would get better and advised me to keep reading. I tried but it continued to be just as bad.

I remembered the sentence from the gospel where Jesus said: "Everyone therefore who acknowledges me before others, I also will acknowledge before my Father in heaven" (Mt 10:32). If I really loved God, I thought, then I had to follow his teaching and speak up. When I spoke with my professor again about how reading this book went against my conscience, he laughed at me. At the start of the next class, knowing that I hadn't, he gave a quiz to make sure that everyone had done the assignment.

Instead of turning in a blank piece of paper, I wrote the truth — that I respected him, that I wanted to do well in class but that I could not read this book because I felt it was destroying something

I was trying to build within myself. I asked him to respect me as I respected him and allow me to do another assignment. When we got our papers back, he had written on mine: "Okay, I understand. Don't worry about doing another assignment."

Things changed from that point on. When I began working on my semester project, I tried to work with him, asking for his thoughts about my ideas. When I presented the paper, he seemed very happy with it and gave me an "A." The next semester, I decided to take another class offered by the same professor. He had included in the course description a section on mutual respect, which he asked the students to have for one another and for him, and he promised to do the same.

Theresa, Indiana

"*Faith ... in some ways is reason itself guided by God, in an ecstasy of cognitive love, outside of self, remaining what it is but permeated by Christ.*"

Giuseppe Maria Zanghi[11]

6.

The Need for Relationships

"If all people, or at least even a very small group of persons were true servants of God in their 'neighbor,' soon the world would belong to Christ.... The simple eye sees in each person 'a Christ coming to be.' It places self at the service of all ... so that Christ may emerge and grow in them. It sees in each person a Christ being born, who must grow, live, do good, a new child of God who must die, rise, and be glorified.... The soul must give itself no peace until, through its continual service, it recognizes in its brother or sister the spiritual features of Christ."

Chiara Lubich[1]

"Side by side with the collective proclamation of the Gospel, the other form of transmission, the person-to-person one, remains valid and important. The Lord often used it (for example, with Nicodemus, Zacchaeus, the Samaritan woman, Simon the Pharisee), and so did the apostles.... It must not happen that the pressing need to proclaim the Good News to the multitudes should cause us to forget this form of proclamation whereby an individual's personal conscience

is reached and touched by an entirely unique word that he receives from someone else."

Paul VI[2]

"Above all, that of which we are in need at this moment in history are men who, through an enlightened and lived faith, render God credible in this world. The negative testimony of Christians who speak about God and live against him, has darkened God's image and opened the door to disbelief. We need men who have their gaze directed to God, to understand true humanity. We need men whose intellects are enlightened by the light of God, and whose hearts God opens, so that their intellects can speak to the intellects of others, and so that their hearts are able to open up to the hearts of others. Only through men who have been touched by God, can God come near to men."

Joseph Cardinal Ratzinger[3]

"Look outside yourself, not in yourself, not in things, not in persons; look at God outside of yourself in order to unite yourself to him."

"He lives in the depths of every soul that is alive and, if dead, the soul is the tabernacle of God that awaits him as the joy and expression of its own existence."

"Look at every neighbor then with love, and love means to give. A gift, moreover, calls for a gift and you will be loved in return."

"Understood in this way, love is to love and be loved, as in the Trinity."

"God in you will ravish hearts, igniting the life of the Trinity in them, which may already rest in them through grace, although extinguished."

Chiara Lubich [4]

Loving Your Neighbor as Yourself

"In this life we cannot do great things. We can only do small things with great love."

Mother Teresa of Calcutta [5]

In our business, we try to see competitors not as the ones to beat, but as people with whom we can build relationships. Since we started, we have tried to follow the principle of never speaking ill of a competitor. It's tempting when someone calls seeking negative information about them, but we refrain. We compete only by the quality of our product and our service. We have even helped people in our area to start similar companies, sharing with them how we started, how to avoid the mistakes that we made, and sending along résumés of good people when they don't serve our own employment needs.

Also, when asked to testify in court, it is tempting to go on about a competitor's mistakes. But I try to make it a point to also say what they did right. We saw one result of building these kinds of relationships when we were involved in a fairly large bid for a sophisticated project in another state. When the attorney for the city stood up to say how our references checked out, he confessed that he had spoken not only with our client referrals, but also with our competitors. "I tried to get the dirt on this company, to find out what they do not do well, and I have never heard such glowing remarks from competitors. I have no reservations about hiring these people."

Matthew, Indiana

"As necessary and useful as they can be, the best of structures are not enough – organizations, economic and technical means, pastoral programs, documents and study. Only deep gospel life generates true evangelization."
Pasquale Foresi[6]

Blessed are the Peacemakers

"Now there is a final reason I think that Jesus says, 'Love your enemies.' It is this: that love has within it a redemptive power. And there is a power there that eventually transforms individuals.... That's love, you see. It is redemptive, and this is why Jesus says love. There's something about love that builds up and is creative."
Martin Luther King, Jr.[7]

Our school district, finding itself in a difficult financial situation, was considering whether to close my daughter's elementary school. Initially the district opened the doors for people to propose alternatives and solutions, but quickly the discussion became a polarized battle that dominated the local TV, the newspapers and the Internet.

At first I wanted to join one of the "fronts," but then I recognized that regardless of my feelings about the situation, my job was to build bridges between the concerned parents, the schools, and the board of education.

I realized that the first step was to try to open the lines of communication. I scheduled an appointment with a member of the board, hoping to see things from their perspective. I was a little nervous when I realized that the people who would meet with me were the ones I found it hardest to communicate with!

So that morning I decided that the sole purpose of my going was to listen and to love them. The meeting went on for several hours. I did very little talking and for the most part just listened.

In the end, I had established a positive relationship with one of the members, which eventually blossomed into a beautiful friendship — to the point that she has even helped me with a job hunt.

Establishing lines of communication with the other members of the board was more difficult, but eventually we were able to work together on some issues.

At a certain point, I met the mayor of our town, who was so touched by the turnaround in attitudes on this polarizing issue that he came to our house for dinner and wants to continue to learn about this approach.

For all of us, it was a chance to build relationships that bridge all kinds of differences. Who would ever have thought this could come out of a school-closing debate!

Heather, New Jersey

Loving in the Truth

"Let no one ever come to you without leaving better and happier."
Mother Teresa of Calcutta[8]

M y mother and father taught us the value of honesty and integrity in school. But I have sometimes found myself in conflict, especially for the simplest things, like not letting other students copy my homework. My classmates would come to me sometimes because they had forgotten to do their homework or because they couldn't understand a problem. I would think: "They are my friends. How could I not help them?" Sometimes I would give in and slip them a few answers, but each time I would dread the feeling I had inside because — even if it was so insignificant, or if I did it just once in a while — dishonesty was dishonesty. I hated cheating and letting others cheat off of me.

One day, risking mockery from my friends, I finally told them how I felt and talked to them about this issue in light of the gospel values that I try to live. To my surprise, my friends actually seemed to understand my reasoning. Now, they come up to me not to cheat, but to ask how to do something or even to tell me that they finished their homework on their own! Doing their own homework, they are doing better in our classes.

Laura, Texas

Give and It Shall Be Given to You

"Courage is needed: the courage of one's convictions; the courage to be close to others; the courage to live in a contemplative mode and the courage to serve with simplicity and humility; the courage to scale Mount Tabor and the courage to wash the feet of one's neighbor."

Bishop Klaus Hemmerle[9]

A short while ago, my husband found out that a relative was in credit card trouble. Although he was paying his monthly fees, his finance charges were making him sink deeper and deeper into debt (about $7,000). Considering that the interest rate on loans is much lower than the credit card fees, we thought we could take out extra loans for his relative to pay off his credit card.

I have to be honest; at first I was a little hesitant. That was a lot of money.

"With the baby coming, who knows if we will need that money?" I thought. "What if he doesn't pay us back? The loans we take out are in our name, so we're responsible."

But I felt that it was the right thing to do. The Gospel says, "Strive first for the kingdom of God ..." (Mt 6:33). Money was very tight, but we went ahead with the loan.

Just a few weeks later, we found out that my husband had received a scholarship for $26,000 — almost four times the amount we had given his relative. The money has no strings attached, and we don't have to pay anything back to the school.

At first, we didn't even believe it. My husband went to talk to the admissions department at the university to be sure of the scholarship's terms, but it was, in fact, free. God really does provide. For us this was the hundredfold promised by the gospel.

Terri, California

"But we ... neither feed Him when hungry, nor clothe Him when naked, but seeing Him begging, we pass him by. And yet if ye saw [Christ] Himself, every one would strip himself of all his goods. But even now it is the same. For He Himself has said, I am he."

St. John Chrysostom[10]

Loving Everyone

"Never lose sight that whenever you are not loving your neighbor, the good God is furious with you."

St. John Vianney[11]

The long history of conflict between Iran and Iraq has caused both sides to look down on each other. In one of my lab classes, I noticed that one of my classmates was struggling with the lab assignment. Normally I like helping others without hesitation. But this classmate was an Iranian, and I hesitated to approach her because I thought she would look down on me just because I'm an Iraqi.

However, I decided to help her, notwithstanding the hatred I grew up with when I lived in Iraq and other Middle Eastern countries.

After class, she invited me for lunch with her friends — all Iranians!! Frankly, I was shocked, but I accepted the invitation. As I got to know her and her friends more, I introduced myself as an Iraqi, and they accepted me as myself.

During the conversation, my classmate told me that she didn't like the conflict between Iraq and Iran, and she was convinced that there must be good Iraqi people. When I had decided to help her, she was shocked, too; she had never imagined receiving help from an Iraqi.

I was happy, because I had made a step in taking down the barriers of hatred between Iraqis and Iranians.

Sahir, Ontario

"Forgetting our own suffering, let us plunge into loving humanity present in the neighbor next to us, so that we may gather into our heart the sufferings of the whole human family."

Chiara Lubich[12]

7.

Living Cells of Christianity

"The Church, as 'community of love,' is called to reflect the glory of God's love, and thus attract persons and peoples to Christ. In practicing the unity desired by Jesus, the men and women of our time feel they are invited as they undertake the marvelous adventure of faith. 'That they also may be in us, that the world may believe' (Jn 17:21). The church grows not by proselytizing but by attraction: as Christ attracts all to himself with the power of his love. The church attracts when it lives in communion, for the disciples of Jesus will be recognized if they love one another as He loved us (cf. Rom 12:4-13; Jn 13:34)."

Aparecida Conference[1]

The laity *"gather into smaller groups for serious conversation without any more formal kind of establishment or organization, so that an indication of the community of the Church is always apparent to others as a true witness of love. In this way, by giving spiritual help to one another through friendship and the communicating of the benefit of their experience, they are trained to overcome the disadvan-*

Chapter 7

tages of excessively isolated life and activity and to make their apostolate more productive."

Second Vatican Council[2]

"God who is in me, who has shaped my soul, who lives there as Trinity, is also in the heart of my brothers and sisters.... Therefore, my cell, as the souls intimate with God would say, and my heaven, as we would say, is within me and, just as it is within me, it is in the soul of my brothers and sisters. And just as I love him in me, recollecting myself in this heaven – when I am alone – I love him in my brother or sister when he or she is close to me. And so I no longer love only silence, but also the word: the communication between God in me with God in my brother or sister.... We must give life continuously to these living cells of the Mystical Body of Christ – who are brothers ad sisters united in his name – in order to revive the whole Body."

Chiara Lubich[3]

"When we make ourselves one with one or more brothers or sisters in the name of Jesus, then Jesus rushes in mystically among them.... I, my neighbor, Jesus: in this triad the very love of the Trinity circulates since in the one who loves Jesus descends and dwells with the Father and with the Holy Spirit. This can happen at home or in the café, in the office

or in the laboratory, in the hospital or in the town square....
Every time there is unity among two or more Christians the
presence of Jesus is released

Igino Giordani[4]

"Obviously everyone should be as competent as possible in
their field.... There is the need for men and women who
know how to do this while following the spirit; living and
bringing about unity wherever they are, and thereby allow-
ing Jesus in the midst to manifest himself. It is only in that
way that we know how to follow God's plans, surely the
most effective and quickest for bringing about the renewal
of humanity."

Pasquale Foresi[5]

Building Bridges of Love

*"Your neighbor is not someone you know, someone who is a friend
or relative. Your neighbor is whoever has need of you."*

Jean Vanier[6]

O ur neighborhood has the annual tradition of a block party.
We have a great variety of neighbors, from retired couples
in their eighties to young singles in their twenties. For the
past twelve years or so we've taken it upon ourselves to help organize this event.

As can be expected, the fact that people have many ideas can
add variety to the planning, but may also lead to controversy. One
of our neighbors, Ms. Jones, has very strong ideas. Even when
most others disagree with her or have ideas of their own, she has
insisted upon doing things her way. For example, a couple of years
ago she decided that we should hire a disc jockey she knew. As it
turned out, his music was so deafening that by eight o'clock every-
body had left the street because no one could carry on a conversation.

One particular experience a year later presented us with the opportunity to love in spite of division, trying to help everyone work
together. The residents agreed that we would hire a well-known
caller to lead a family square dance. Ms. Jones had wanted to repeat the prior year's musical program and the square dance was
not her idea, so she made other plans for herself that night, leaving her children behind with a baby-sitter. We tried to help them
participate in the various events, and in addition we had agreed to
look after and feed the children of several other families whose
parents were not able to be there. As it turned out the square dance
was a tremendous success. There were grandparents dancing with
their own and other people's two- and three-year-old grandchil-
dren. The neighborhood children had a wonderful time; everyone
participated and no one was left out.

In the end everyone was happy with that year's block party and even weeks later still were talking about how wonderful it had been. When Ms. Jones heard all this, she came to thank us for helping so many have such a good time.

The following year Ms. Jones once again presented an idea with which few agreed. This time, though, she pitched in just the same and contributed to the plan that everyone else wanted, giving her full support. Over the years we have entertained ourselves in a variety of ways. There are now even family talent shows for everyone on the block.

Peter and Irene, Arkansas

"To sum up all in one word – what the soul is in the body, Christians are in the world."

Letter to Diognetus[7]

People before Protocol

"Wherever Christ sees two or three gathered in the faith in his name, he goes there and is present in their midst, drawn by their faith and moved by their oneness of mind."

Origen[8]

As a nurse in a large teaching hospital, my job is to review the protocol documents for all the clinical trials of medicines that we conduct to ensure that they are clearly written and will be implemented safely.

During the review of a new research protocol, we were having a disagreement about whether it would be safe to execute it in the way it was presented to us by a certain new biotech company. Some people worried that the new drug's description and label was going to be confusing to the pharmacists preparing the drug and the nurses administering it. A pharmacist and I felt strongly that it was going to be unsafe, even though some physician colleagues felt it was fine. Without our agreement, however, the protocol could not go forward.

Initially, the drug company was adamant about not wanting to change anything, saying that the Food and Drug Administration had approved the protocol and the drug labeling. I had also heard that this company was well known for being difficult to work with. Thus no one was expecting that the protocol would be changed, but we weren't willing to compromise what we thought would impact patient safety.

It turned out, however, that the drug company was very interested in working with us and finally proposed some changes to the protocol. When our principal investigator sent an email with this news, I quickly replied "Alleluia!" This set off a chain of polarizing emails that widened the gap with our physician colleagues.

I felt tempted to say nothing, to not stick my neck out and hope that time would cool things off. I could have just stayed quiet, happy that my pharmacist friend and I had succeeded in making the protocol safer, and leave it at that. But I felt that this was a chance for me to re-establish dialogue with our physician colleagues, helping all of us focus on the commitment which I know we all share.

First of all, I apologized if my email had sounded like I had won a victory. I explained that I did not see the biotech company as the enemy and that I thought all of us, including drug companies, were seeking to work together to provide the best treatments that science can offer in the safest possible way.

I then offered to help preview future protocols while they were being drafted, so that any potential problems could be worked out ahead of time. We would all use our time more efficiently if we revised the protocols while they were still in the writing process.

I was hoping to show my willingness to help and that I did not intend to introduce stumbling blocks to the work.

This seemed to cool things off right away, and the accusatory emails stopped. The next day my boss told me that I had done a good job not only in ensuring the safety of those patients who would enroll in this clinical trial but also in calming the waters and showing my willingness to collaborate. It was a positive reflection not only on me but also on our department.

We continued working with this drug company. The protocol was eventually approved by the Institutional Review Board, the committee that approves all research on people and of which I am a member. The trial has been open to enrollment without mishaps so far, because of the safety measures we had put in place from the start.

Our relationships have continued to be collegial, and my pharmacist friend and I are now being consulted on new protocols that are being considered.

Evelyn, Massachusetts

> "We ourselves feel that what we are doing is just a drop in the ocean. But the ocean would be less because of that missing drop."
>
> Mother Teresa of Calcutta[9]

Touching Hearts

"Brother helped by brother is like a strong city."

St. John Chrysostom[10]

I am a chiropractor, and my interaction with colleagues, teaching at seminars, and work in my practice are motivated by the idea of living the gospel call to mutual love. Some colleagues and I bring this common effort to our staff meetings and notice that, as a consequence, the rest of our office members also become part of this atmosphere of unity.

A staff member was having a difficult time with one of our patients. This patient would call at the last minute for appointments and then show up late, forcing us to work overtime. When she arrived, she would want immediate attention and often seemed irritated. This caused the staff to become more and more anxious about interacting with her. They began to dread hearing her voice on the phone.

One day we discussed this at the staff meeting. We all agreed to accept this patient unconditionally, to treat her with dignity by consciously choosing not to react to her demanding attitude.

As a result, the staff took a decisive step to be open to this patient. Many times when she came to the office late and in a huff, the bookkeeper would invite her into her office to sit down, and after being listened to for a while the patient would calm down. I also made an effort to be more loving and understanding with her, listening to her complaints as I would want to be listened to.

Not only did she start coming on time but she actually called the office one day to see if she could arrive an hour earlier just to sit in the waiting room to do some work because she felt "so peaceful there."

I had been taking care of this patient for months and felt that she had not made any significant progress. I had discussed this case with colleagues who had also treated her. They agreed that she had not been going forward in her care. But the love that she experienced while with us made it possible for her to drop her defenses and opened her up to receive a greater depth of healing. Recently she said to me, "I have never felt so cared for and embraced as I do by you and your entire staff."

Other patients have remarked on the peaceful atmosphere in our office and on how they feel better as soon as they walk in the door. I realize that they are feeling the presence of Jesus generated by our effort to love every person who comes for treatment.

Brian, Georgia

> "Since God is three Persons in one, and this cannot but be reflected in all of creation, we should learn to see things always in their relatedness, and to walk together, to live in unity."
>
> Fr. Tony Weber[11]

Building a Relationship

> "The Church is the event of loving one another."
>
> St. Bonaventure[12]

Just after I was ordained a priest, I worked for a few years in the chancery office with the bishop until I became a pastor in a small town. I had heard that it was a difficult parish in a very divided community.

I arrived wanting to serve the parishioners but, above all, to build a relationship with the other priest there, who wasn't very communicative. The first days we sat down for dinner I would try to start a conversation, but he would only mumble an answer, and I realized it wasn't going to be easy. I decided to do my best to convey that above all I cared about him as a human being.

Even though I was the pastor, he had more years of experience, which could have caused friction between us. I tried to include him in all the decisions affecting parish life and convince him and all the committed parishioners that we shared the responsibilities of the parish. I tried to be attentive to the details of life by informing him of my daily schedule or by making available the better of our cars, especially when he had to make long trips or use rough roads.

After a while, I realized that he was devoted to pastoral work and faithful to his commitments, but because of his reserved nature, he gave the appearance of being difficult. Little by little I discovered the treasure hidden within him.

Our relationship really improved. He appreciated my trust and began to share his daily schedule, his worries and his plans. Many people in the parish were edified by the relationship of charity between us, and our parish was becoming more and more united.

Our three years together were an experience of human and spiritual growth for both of us. He then became pastor of another parish. I realized once more that practical and personal love is the key to building unity among priests, in the parish community and in the world.

Fr. Roberto, Dominican Republic

"Strive, therefore, in every parish ... to restore life to the small groups or counseling centers for the faithful who proclaim Christ and his word, places where it is possible to experience faith, to put charity into practice and to organize hope."

Benedict XVI[13]

Healing Racial Tensions

The "messianic people ... is nonetheless a lasting and sure seed of unity, hope and salvation."

Second Vatican Council [14]

One Friday afternoon, my eight-year-old Diana came off the school bus very upset. During the ride home, a seventh-grade boy had made insulting comments about African Americans, and other children had chimed in.

My older daughter and I were incredibly angered by this and tried to comfort Diana by reminding her how special she is, being bi-racial. It seemed evident to all of us that we had to embrace this suffering and live up to our commitment to the gospel. We had to love even this boy.

On Monday morning, I sent an email to the principal, detailing the things that were said to Diana on the bus. He immediately called me and shared his plan to speak with Diana and the boy. He reprimanded the boy, had him apologize to Diana, and suspended him from school for several days.

The principal asked if I would like to speak to the boy and his parents before he was scheduled to return to school after his suspension. I saw this as an opportunity to build a relationship with this family. Diana and I prayed together and then decided to do three things at the meeting: One, show the boy love and forgiveness. Two, educate the boy as to who Diana really is and where she comes from, because addressing the truth is also love. Three, promise to become an example to the other children of how two kids who are expected to dislike each other (he had said nasty things, and she got him into trouble) can still show each other kindness and prove they can go beyond the incident.

The day of the meeting arrived. As Diana and I walked down the hall holding hands, I felt a special love accompanying us, as

81

if Jesus were present among us, even knowing things might not go the way we hoped. Her little hand gave me enormous strength. The boy and his mother, along with Diana and I, waited together in the front office. I overheard his mother say under her breath that this would be trouble, and I really felt the challenge to live the plan Diana and I agreed to. Sensing the other mother's hostility, Diana declined to go in with me. I sat directly across from the boy's mother, and as I shared every point we wanted to make, I watched her expression change from embarrassment and defensiveness to acceptance. She was obviously surprised to hear something positive from me. At the conclusion of the meeting, the boy shook my hand and promised to try to be an example. When I went back to work, I received a beautiful email from the principal: "Thank you again for your gracious response and understanding of this incident and for those kind and uplifting words to the other family. I was very touched. Please know that I am at your service and that I look forward to seeing you again under happier circumstances."

During the last week of school, the boy saw Diana's big birthday pin on her jumper, and greeted her with a "Happy Birthday." She then reached into her backpack and gave him the last birthday doughnut. They were really friends in the end.

Teresa, New Jersey

> "*If a non-violent person exists, a non-violent family must exist. If a non-violent family exists, why not a non-violent village, city, country and world?*"
>
> Mahatma Gandhi[15]

8.

The One Human Family

"*The Church must enter into dialogue with the world in which it lives. It has something to say, a message to give, a communication to make.*"

"*We rejoice and find great consolation in the fact that this dialogue, both inside and outside the Church, has already begun. The Church today is more alive than ever before. But when we weigh the matter more closely we see that there is still a great way to go. In fact the work which is beginning today will never come to an end. This is a law of our earthly, time-bound pilgrimage.*"

Paul VI[1]

"*No one, in principle, is unreachable; in principle, all people can and must be reached. For the Catholic Church, no one is a stranger, no one is excluded, no one is far away.*"

Paul VI[2]

"*Respect and love ought to be extended also to those who think or act differently than we do in social, political and even religious matters. In fact, the more deeply we come to understand their ways of thinking through such courtesy and love, the more easily will we be able to enter into dialogue with them. This love and good will, to be sure, must in no way render us indifferent to truth and goodness. Indeed love itself impels the disciples of Christ to speak the saving truth to all.*"

Paul VI[3]

"*The image of the 'Courtyard of the Gentiles' serves as a further element in our thinking on the 'new evangelization' by showing that the Christian must never forgo a sense of boldness in proclaiming the Gospel and seeking every positive way to provide avenues for dialogue, where people's deepest expectations and their thirst for God can be discussed. This boldness allows the question of God to be placed in context through one's sharing of personal experiences in seeking God and recounting the gratuitous nature of the personal encounter with the Gospel of Jesus Christ.*"

Lineamenta for the 2012 Synod of Bishops[4]

"*Since Jesus said that he did not come to be served, but to serve ... we are the servants and the others are the mas-*

ters. *Therefore, it is the brother or sister who has the first word, who is to be honored, obeyed because it is they who command. So then, what is our attitude in relationship to them? ... to put ourselves at their service; to approach them completely empty of ourselves.... In that way the brother or sister can reveal their inner selves, because they have found someone who welcomes them: they can share themselves. But, since the 'emptiness' in us is an 'emptiness of love,' and certainly not an emptiness synonymous with nothingness, the Holy Spirit, who is watching over us, enlightens us and ... enables us to welcome whatever is 'alive' in the heart of the brother or sister, 'alive' in the supernatural sense, a little flame of divine life in them; or 'alive' simply in the human sense, that is, an expression of those values that the Lord, in creating us, has sowed in every human soul. And into that something which is 'alive' we can – by serving – instill with kindness, with love, with unlimited discretion, those aspects of the truth of the gospel message that we carry within us; and those aspects will give fullness and completeness to all that the brother or sister has, believes and is often waiting, even longing for – aspects that draw with them, then, the whole truth."*

Chiara Lubich[5]

Chapter 8

Sharing Gifts: Christian-Muslim Friendship

"Human hearts are yearning for a world where love endures, where gifts are shared, where unity is built, where freedom finds meaning in truth, and where identity is found in respectful communion. Our faith can respond to these expectations."

Benedict XVI[6]

Many times during my career I have worked alongside people of other religions. But there is one individual who became a friend. We shared more than work experiences; we shared family and faith experiences. He was a Muslim who would openly admit that he was lax in the practice of his faith. His wife was a Christian but also did not attend church regularly.

They both loved God and their neighbor and displayed that through their lives. We knew each other well, and he knew of my commitment to my faith and my practice of going to Mass regularly.

One day he said to me, "I wish I prayed more, but five times a day and at work, it's hard." I responded, "Why don't you try to pray at least twice a day for now and then more later?"

He liked the idea, and I helped him find the direction of Mecca from the office.

He and his wife were having trouble in their marriage, and he asked me for help. Being Catholic, I referred him to a priest. They both went to counseling and more than ten years later are still together.

One day we had a discussion about a problem he had with a man whom he felt had done him wrong. He wanted to get back at him and wanted my advice on the best way to do that. We discussed it, but he was taken aback a little by my suggestion of ways to love the offender and let God right it.

"That is why I would never make a good Christian," he said.

"You don't have to be a good Christian, only a good Muslim," I replied. He thanked me and later shared how the problem had a positive outcome.

He has helped me, too. During Ramadan, he shared some of his successes and failures, but explained his belief in the grace of God. This gave me something to think about as we celebrated our Lenten season about the same time that year.

My efforts at fasting and abstinence were nothing compared to Muslim practices. He made me a better Christian as I examined my conscience in repentance and in giving everything to God.

Edward, Texas

*"For by His incarnation the Son of God has united Himself
in some fashion with every man....Christ died for all men,
and the ultimate vocation of man is in fact one, and divine."*
Second Vatican Council [7]

Giving and Finding Joy

*"I offer my life for all of you, but all for humanity that is suffering,
for the young people of my neighborhood, and for all those whom
I have met."*
Carlo Grisolia[8]

It was Christmas and with my mother I was riding home on my bicycle. On the way I saw a cell phone lying on the ground, so I picked it up and gave it to her.

Chapter 8

As soon as we reached home, I took out the SIM card and put in my own. My mother said, "Son, you should give the phone back to its owner. Who knows how worried he is, and he might be more in need of it than are we." I replied, "Mother, I found it, I didn't steal it."

Suddenly, the words of Jesus flashed in my mind: "Whatever you do to the least of my brothers you do unto me."

My mother said, "Learn to give joy to others with your life." Then, I thought, I should make my mother happy and God will be happy with me, too.

I took out my SIM card, replaced it with that of the owner and switched on the cell phone.

A few minutes later, I received a call from the boy who had lost it. He was a rickshaw driver, about twenty years old. I told him to come to a stop close to our house to pick it up. When I gave his cell phone back to him, he said, "I am a poor boy and had bought it with great effort."

He was very happy to find his lost phone. He, a Muslim, said, "If you were not a Christian, I might not have gotten it back again"

I felt profound joy and peace when I heard this, and I experienced new faith that if we give joy to others we ourselves feel joy.

Reginald, Pakistan

"Let us try to open our eyes to the neighbors we meet, to appreciate the good they do, whatever their convictions may be, to feel solidarity with them and encourage one another in the way of justice and of love."

Chiara Lubich[9]

Reaching Out

"We have learned to fly the air like birds and swim the sea like fish, but we have not yet learned the simple art of living together as brothers."

Martin Luther King, Jr.[10]

Some years ago we moved into our present home, situated on a small court in Toronto's West End. We decided that the best way to get to know our neighbors was to invite them over, one family at a time. This has led to a warm rapport among us. As time went on, the fruit of these small actions of openness was our beginning to help one another in times of need, helping us to become even closer to one another.

An important day for us is July 1, when we celebrate Canada Day, a national holiday, the date in 1867 when our country was constitutionally established as a nation. Each year, government and local municipalities sponsor many festivities. Our neighborhood group decided to celebrate this special day together by taking turns hosting an annual BBQ. We've been doing this for about 10 years now, and it has helped to create a sense of family among us. We experienced great joy in planting this little seed of a united world in our local community.

Then we decided it was time to go a step further, to venture beyond our small street and to have a summer ice cream social. We invited the neighbors on the adjacent streets, along with family and friends. We wanted our invitations to be personal, so we delivered them by hand. The barriers that appeared to be between us seemed to come down. We were warmly welcomed, and each person wanted to get to know the others better.

In the summer of 2011, more than 60 neighbors participated — young and old alike. Although the invitation was to have ice cream together, it turned into a meal since everyone brought food to share as well. The joy on our street was tangible. We even had a mini-orchestra, an international group with an accordion player, guitarist and drummer. We all enjoyed spontaneous singing and dancing. The atmosphere that was built throughout the evening was one of intimate dialogue, with people sharing their personal stories.

As we reflected later on all that has happened over these years, we realized the importance of having planted that first small seed of mutual love many years ago. It was a beginning step, but today we have a neighborhood where we live in harmony. We share both good and difficult moments together, and neighborhood family news circulates regularly.

We too have been enriched as we discovered each person's values and how much they want to give in different ways. One of our neighbors had heard about a family who needed furniture and immediately offered his own dining room set, still in excellent condition. In other neighborhoods, we know that doesn't happen too often.

We particularly enjoy the moments in our day when we meet each other on the street or in the store. The good feeling comes from knowing that now we have something that connects us. It's really true that you only need a small spark of love to begin to create a new community. We feel we are doing our best to build a new city from our own little corner of the world.

Xavier and Nora, Ontario

> "Catholics should try to cooperate with all men and women of good will to promote whatever is true, whatever just, whatever holy, whatever lovable (cf. Phil 4:8). They should hold discussions with them, excel them in prudence and courtesy, and initiate research on social and public practices which should be improved in line with the spirit of the Gospel."
>
> Second Vatican Council[11]

Loving Until the End

"We must ... see others, without exception, as candidates for unity."
Chiara Lubich[12]

I had been working at a bank for over twenty-five years with my boss, Luke. One day, he complained of feeling fatigue and general malaise. Since his son's wedding was approaching, his wife insisted he get a checkup so he underwent extensive medical consultations and tests. Days later, I answered a call. It was his doctor, so I handed him the phone; after listening for a few moments he hung up, then nearly collapsed. He did not tell me anything but left the office immediately. I presumed he was headed home, so I invented some pretext to call his wife, insisting that she meet him at the train station. A biopsy the next day revealed a stage four cancer. He agreed to have one chemo treatment, so as to attend his son's wedding.

What followed was excruciating for him. His family was in pieces, our coworkers incredulous, our former banking community stunned. I was in constant contact with both Luke and his wife. On first hearing the diagnosis I was left speechless, but later did muster up the courage to say, "Luke, this is a moment of God for you." Although he was not the religious type, he acknowledged with "Yes it is." That evening in a commentary I read something which touched me: a gospel sentence, "Walk according to the Spirit of the Lord," followed by the mention of love of neighbor. So I began to live it, asking and praying for Luke. The closer I followed his situation, the more I began to notice a change in him. To be sure he was filled with fear and in pain, but at the same time I saw not mere resignation, but an acceptance of this illness. He also spoke often of what he had accomplished in life with his family and in his career.

Fifty days had passed since that dreadful telephone call. It was a hot July day. The CFO of our firm had arrived from Europe and I accompanied him to the hospital to see Luke. I felt numb at seeing how the disease had consumed him — once such a handsome man and still only 58 years old. Yet his eyes were full of life. As I entered the hospital room that morning, another Bible sentence came to mind: "The Lord is near to all who call upon him" (Ps 145:18).

Luke acknowledged us and we spoke to him; he gathered enough energy to say a word or two: "I am so happy to see you both." Before leaving I kissed his forehead and whispered, "Thank you Luke for everything and don't worry, what's inside is so beautiful." Five days later, he died.

Still today I am in contact with Luke's wife and we often speak about him. He had returned to the sacraments during his illness and during his final days he often said he was no longer part of this world. And as immobile and weak as we was, he always asked for a crucifix to hold in hand.

Tammy, New York

"I go in search not for the devout, but for the most lost and desperate."

St. Francis de Geronimo[13]

Afterword

If a City Were Set On Fire

If a city were set alight at various points, even by small fires, but they managed to resist being put out, soon the city would be aflame. If a city, in the most different places, were lit up by the fire that Jesus brought on earth, and this fire, through the good-will of the people who lived there, managed to resist the ice of the world, we would soon have the city aflame with the love of God.

The fire that Jesus brought to earth is himself. It is charity: love which not only binds the soul to God, but also souls to one another. In fact, a lighted supernatural fire means the continual triumph of God in souls who have given themselves to him and, because they are united to him, united among themselves.

Two or more people fused in the name of Christ, who are not afraid or ashamed to declare explicitly to one another their desire to love God, but who actually make of this unity in Christ their Ideal, are a divine power in the world.

And in every city these souls could spring up in families: father and mother, son and father, mother and mother-in-law. They could meet in parishes, in associations, in social bodies, in schools, in offices, everywhere. It is not necessary for them to be saints already, or Jesus would have said so. It is enough for them to be united in the name of Christ and that they never go back on this unity.

Naturally, they will not remain two or three for very long, for charity spreads of itself and grows by enormous proportions. Every small cell, set alight by God in any point of the earth, will necessarily spread, and Providence will distribute these flames, these souls on fire, wherever it thinks fit, so that the world in many places may be restored to the warmth of the love of God, and hope again.

Chiara Lubich[1]

93

Notes

Foreword

1. In *The Modern Philosophical Revolution: The Luminosity of Existence,* New York: Cambridge University Press, 2008. Philosophers mentioned include: Kant, Hegel and Schelling, Kierkegaard, Nietzsche and Heidegger, Levinas and Derrida.
2. The Apostolic Exhortation *Christifideles Laici* (The Vocation and Mission of the Lay Faithful in the Church and in the World), 30 December 1988, n. 34.
3. John Paul II, Apostolic Letter at the beginning of the new millennium, *Novo Millennio Ineunte,* 6 January 2001, n. 56, http://www.vatican.va/holy_father/john_paul_ii/apost_letters/documents/hf_jp-ii_apl_20010106_novo-millennio-ineunte_en.html.
4. Benedict XVI, Apostolic Exhortation on the Word of God in the life and mission of the Church, *Verbum Domini,* 30 September 2010, n. 94, http://www.vatican.va/holy_father/benedict_xvi/apost_exhortations/documents/hf_ben-xvi_exh_20100930_verbum-domini_en.html.
5. See Chiara Lubich, *May They All Be One* (London: New City, 1977), 37.

1. Genuine Gospel Life

1. *The Second Epistle of Clement,*.13, http://www.earlychristianwritings.com/text/2clement-roberts.html.
2. *Evangelii Nuntiandi* (On Evangelization in the Modern World), 76. http://www.vatican.va/holy_father/paul_vi/apost_exhortations/documents/hf_p-vi_exh_19751208_evangelii-nuntiandi_en.html.
3. Ibid.
4. Chiara Favotti, ed., *Una Buona Notizia* (Rome: Citta' Nuova, 2012), 25. Editors' translation.
5. *Markings* (New York: Ballantine, 1983), 134.
6. *Introduction to the Devout Life* (London: Longmans, 1891), 7.
7. "Letter to the Ephesians," 47. In S. H. Shrawley, *The Epistles of St. Ignatius, Bishop of Antioch* (New York: Macmillan, 1919).

8. In Malcom Muggeridge, *Something Beautiful for God* (New York: Harper and Row, 1986), 67.
9. In Eva Pennington, *One Year Alone with God: 366 Devotions on the Names of God* (Grand Rapids MI: Baker, 2010), 208.
10. Favotti, 29. Editors' translation.
11. *Essential Writings* (Hyde Park NY: New City Press, 2007), 190.
12. Nineteenth-century German poet, translator, and professor of Oriental languages. Cited in Favotti, 31. Editors' translation.
13. The motto chosen for an international youth festival, "Genfest 2012," taken from her commentary for the November 1997 Word of Life. See http://www.genfest.org/stepsto/You-wont-be-at-peace-until-broken-relationships-even-for-something-small-are-healed.

2. Guided by the Word

1. *Essential Writings,* 7.
2. Homily, Chrism Mass in St. Peter's Basilica, Holy Thursday, 9 April 2009. http://www.vatican.va/holy_father/benedict_xvi/homilies/2009/documents/hf_ben-xvi_hom_20090409_messa-crismale_en.html.
3. *Essential Writings,* 127.
4. *Insegnamenti di Paolo VI,* Volume V (Vatican: Libreria Editrice Vaticana, 1967), 936-939. Editors' translation.
5. *Libri delle sentenze,* 3, 8-9 (*Patrologia Latina* 83, 679-680), cited in Favotti, 35. Editors' translation.
6. *Vie per l'unità,: Tracce di un cammino teologico e spirituale* (Rome: Città Nuova, Roma 1985), 39,44. Editors' translation.
7. *Tractate in Psalmum,* 13, 1 (*Patrologia Latina* 9, 295), cited in Favotti, 35. Editor's translation
8. Quoted in Chris Anderson, *Edge Effects: Notes from an Oregon Forest* (Iowa City IA: University of Iowa Press, 1993), xv.
9. *Essere tua Parola* (Rome: Città Nuova, 2008), 37. Editors' translation.
10. "Justin Martyr: Philosopher Turned Evangelist," in *History of the Early Church,* http://earlychurch.com/Justin.php.
11. Quoted in Chiara Lubich, *A New Way: The Spirituality of Unity* (Hyde Park NY: New City Press, 2006), 29-30.
12. *Poèmata ad alios* VII (ad Nemesium), vv. 37-49 (*Patrologia Greca* 37, 1553), cited in Favotti, 40. Editors' translation.
13. Homily, Solemnity of the Holy Apostles Peter and Paul, Sunday, 28 June 2010, http://www.vatican.va/holy_father/benedict_xvi/homilies/2010/documents/hf_ben-xvi_hom_20100628_vespri-pietro-paolo_en.html.

3. Rooted in Christ

1. *Evangelii Nuntiandi*, 76.
2. "Renewed Commitment to Proclaim Jesus: Statement of the Symposium *Evangelization in the Light of Ecclesia in Asia*," Pattaya, Thailand, 3-7 September 2002, www.sedosmission.org.
3. Motu Proprio, "Uubicumque et Semper," 21 September 2010, http://www.vatican.va/holy_father/benedict_xvi/apost_letters/documents/hf_ben-xvi_apl_20100921_ubicumque-et-semper_en.html.
4. *Deus Caritas Est*, 7, http://www.vatican.va/holy_father/benedict_xvi/encyclicals/documents/hf_ben-xvi_enc_20051225_deus-caritas-est_en.html.
5. "Dio è vicino," *Scritti Spirituali/4* (Rome: Città Nuova, 1995), 50. Editors' translation.
6. "Va' con la forza che è in te: La figura di Gedeone," *La Civiltà Cattolica*, 1 July 2012, 46. Editors' translation.
7. *La Sainte Eucharistie : La présence réelle* (Paris: Librairie Eucharistique, 1951), 307. Editors' translation.
8. Homily of the Holy Father, Kapellplatz, Altötting, 11 September 2006, http://www.vatican.va/holy_father/benedict_xvi/homilies/2006/documents/hf_ben-xvi_hom_20060911_shrine-altotting_en.html.
9. *Decree on the Apostolate of the Laity*, 3, http://www.vatican.va/archive/hist_councils/ii_vatican_council/documents/vat-ii_decree_19651118_apostolicam-actuositatem_en.html.
10. *Essential Writings*, 80.
11. From an unfinished letter to Br. Alois. Cited in Favotti, 49. Editors' translation.
12. Letter to Priests, Holy Thursday 2002, http://www.vatican.va/holy_father/john_paul_ii/letters/2002/documents/hf_jp-ii_let_20020321_priests-holy-thursday_en.html.

4. The Courage to Speak Up

1. *Evangelii Nuntiandi*, 57.
2. *Novo Millennio Ineunte* (At the Beginning of the New Millennium), 40, http://www.vatican.va/holy_father/john_paul_ii/apost_letters/documents/hf_jp-ii_apl_20010106_novo-millennio-ineunte_en.html.
3. *On the Word of God in the Life and Mission of the Church*, 93, http://www.vatican.va/roman_curia/synod/documents/rc_synod_doc_20080511_instrlabor-xii-assembly_en.html.

4. "To Participants in the Plenary Assembly of the Pontifical Council for Promoting the New Evangelization," 30 May 2011, http://www.vatican.va/holy_father/benedict_xvi/speeches/2011/may/documents/hf_ben-xvi_spe_20110530_nuova-evangelizzazione_en.html.
5. *Essere tua Parola* (Rome: Città Nuova, 2008), 58. Editors' translation.
6. *Evangelii Nuntiandi*, 24.
7. In John McClemon, *Sermon in a Sentence; A Treasury of Quotes on the Spiritual Life from St. Thérèse of Lisieux* (San Francisco: Ignatius Press, 2002), 65.
8. "Pilgrimage to Nonviolence" in *Strength to Love* (1958), http://mlk-kpp01.stanford.edu/index.php/resources/article/king_quotes_on_war_and_peace/.
9. St. Vincent de Paul Quotes, http://www.vinnies.org.au/st-vincent-quotes-nsw.
10. *Decree on the Apostolate of the Laity*, 12.
11. *The Word of God in the Life and Mission of the Church*, 97, http://www.vatican.va/roman_curia/synod/documents/rc_synod_doc_20080511_instrlabor-xii-assembly_en.html.
12. Quoted in The Daily Telegraph, 31 March 2010, http://audienceofone.org.uk/tag/rowan-williams/
13. Larry Chang, ed. *Wisdom for the Soul: Five Millennia of Prescriptions for Spiritual Healing* (Washington: Gnosophia, 2006), 425.
14. *Paradoxes of Faith* (San Francisco, Ignatius Press: 1987), 39.

5. Trustworthy Witness

1. *Evangelii Nuntiandi*, 22.
2. Ibid, 53.
3. "To Participants in the Plenary Assembly of the Pontifical Council for Promoting the New Evangelization," 30 May 2011, http://www.vatican.va/holy_father/benedict_xvi/speeches/2011/may/documents/hf_ben-xvi_spe_20110530_nuova-evangelizzazione_en.html.
4. XIII Ordinary General Assembly: The New Evangelization for the Transmission of the Christian Faith, 22 and 19, http://www.vatican.va/roman_curia/synod/documents/rc_synod_doc_20110202_lineamenta-xiii-assembly_en.html.
5. "Chiedersi a ogni azione che compiamo: sto evangelizzando?" In *Cercando le cose di lassù* (Rome: Città Nuova, 1992), 160. Editors' translation.

6. From a speech to the Bishops Friends of the Focolare Movement, Castelgandolfo (Italy), 7 March 2012.
7. Letter to H. E. Mons. Francis J. Dunn, Auxiliary Bishop of Dubuque, 28 May 1986, http://www.vatican.va/holy_father/john_paul_ii/letters/1986/documents/hf_jp-ii_let_19860528_francis-dunn_en.html.
8. *Commento al Vangelo di S. Marco*, lib. I, Roma 1970, 116-117, cited in Favotti, 64. Editors' translation.
9. Jean-Joseph Huguet, ed., *The Consoling Thoughts of St. Francis de Sales* (Dublin: M.H. Gill and Son, 1877), 92.
10. Quoted by Tim Drake, "The Pope's Forest," in "Symposium 'Light of the World' and Pope Benedict XVI," *Catholic Channel*, http://www.patheos.com/Resources/Additional-Resources/Symposium-Light-of-the-World-and-Pope-Benedict-XVI?offset=4&max=1.
11. *Gesù Abbandonato: Maestro di Pensiero* (Rome: Città Nuova, 2008), 38. Editors' translation.

6. The Need for Relationships

1. *Essential Writings*, 18-19.
2. *Evangelii Nuntiandi*, 46.
3. "Cardinal Ratzinger on Europe's Crisis of Culture"; lecture given at the convent of Saint Scholastica in Subiaco, Italy, 1 April 2005, http://www.catholiceducation.org/articles/politics/pg0143.html
4. *Essential Writings*, 80.
5. Gwen Costello, ed. *Spiritual Gems from Mother Teresa* (New London CT: Bayard, 2008), 14.
6. Favotti, 69. Editors' translation.
7. Clayborne Carson, ed. "Loving Your Enemies," in *A Knock at Midnight: Inspiration from the Great Sermons of Rev. Martin Luther King, Jr.* (New York: Hachette, 2001), e-book.
8. Costello, 19.
9. Unpublished manuscript, "Il Sacerdote Oggi, Il Religioso Oggi," delivered to the International Congress for Priests and Religious, Vatican City, 30 April 1982, 25. Editors' translation.
10. "Homily LXXXVIII, Matthew 27: 45-48," in *The Homilies of St. John Chrysostom, Archbishop of Constantinople on the Gospel of Matthew, Translated, With Notes and Indices, Part III. Homily LIX – XC* (Oxford: John Henry Parker, 1852), 1150.
11. *Scritti Scelti* (Rome: Città Nuova, 1970), 114. Editors' translation.
12. *Detti Gen* (Rome: Città Nuova, 2006), 29. Editors' translation.

7. Living Cells of Christianity

1. Fifth General Conference of the Bishops of Latin America and the Caribbean: Concluding Document, 31 May 2007, paragraph 159, page 63, www.aecrc.org/documents/Aparecida-Concluding%20 Document.doc.
2. *Decree on the Apostolate of the Laity*, 14
3. *Essential Writings, 33-34.*
4. *Il Laico Chiesa* (Rome: Città Nuova, 1988), 142. Editors' translation.
5. *Colloqui* (Rome: Città Nuova, 2009), 112. Editors' translation.
6. Cited in Favottti, 44. Editors' translation.
7. The Epistle of Mathetes to Diognetus, 6, http://www.newadvent.org/fathers/0101.htm.
8. In *Commentarium in Cantica Canticorum*, 41 (*Patrologia Greca* 13, 94), cited in Favotti, 79. Editors' translation.
9. Costello, 30.
10. *St. John Chrysostom on the Priesthood*, B. Harris Cowper, trans. (London: Williams and Norgate, 1866), 16.
11. "Sapienza della Trinità: Alcune Riflesioni sui Distintivi dell' Esperienza Cristiana," http://indaco-torino.net/gens/90_05_06. htm. Editors' translation.
12. *Esamerone* I, 4, cited in Favotti, 82. Editors' translation.
13. Address to the Pastoral Convention of the Diocese of Rome on the Theme: "Church Membership and Pastoral Co-Responsibility," 26 May 2009, http://www.vatican.va/holy_father/benedict_xvi/speeches/2009/may/documents/hf_ben-xvi_spe_20090526_convegno-diocesi-rm_en.html.
14. *Constitution on the Church*, 9, http://www.vatican.va/archive/hist_councils/ii_vatican_council/documents/vat-ii_const_19641121_lumen-gentium_en.html.
15. Cited on website of Genfest 2012, http://www.genfest.org/stepsto/Se-esiste-un-uomo-non-violento-perch-non-pu-esistere-una-famiglia-non-violenta-E-perch-non-un-villaggio-una-citt-un-paese-un-mondo-non-violento-

8. The One Human Family

1. *Ecclesiam Suam* (On The Church), 65 and 117, http://www.vatican.va/holy_father/paul_vi/encyclicals/documents/hf_p-vi_enc_06081964_ecclesiam_en.html.
2. Homily: Closing of the Second Vatican Ecumenical Council, 8 December 1965, http://www.vatican.va/holy_father/paul_vi/

homilies/1965/documents/hf_p-vi_hom_19651208_epilogo-concilio-immacolata_en.html
3. *Evangelii Nuntiandi*, 28.
4. XIII Ordinary General Assembly: "The New Evangelization for the Transmission of the Christian Faith," 5.
5. *Santi Insieme* (Rome: Città Nuova, 1994), 105. Editors' translation.
6. Message of the Holy Father Benedict XVI for the 43rd World Communications Day: "New Technologies, New Relationships. Promoting a Culture of Respect, Dialogue and Friendship," 24 May 2009.
7. *On the Church in the Modern World*, 22, http://www.vatican.va/archive/hist_councils/ii_vatican_council/documents/vat-ii_const_19651207_gaudium-et-spes_en.html.
8. A young man from Genoa who died in 1980 of a brain tumor. He was known for leading a normal life with great holiness. The quotation comes from Favotti, 90. Editors' translation.
9. *Essential Writings*, 355.
10. *Strength to Love* (Minneapolis: Augsburg Fortress, 1981), 75.
11. *Decree on the Apostolate of the Laity*, 14.
12. *The Art of Loving* (Hyde Park NY: New City Press, 2010), 25.
13. In Giovanni Pettinato, *I Santi canonizzati del giorno* (Udine: Edizioni Segno, 1991), 168. Editors' translation.

Afterword

1. *Essential Writings*, 103-04.

Further Reading

All titles are available from New City Press.

www.NewCityPress.com

Neighbors: Short Reflections on Loving the People Around Us
Chiara Lubich, ISBN: 978-1-56548-476-4

Chiara Lubich: A Biography
Armando Torno, ISBN: 978-1-56548-499-5

Early Letters: At the Origins of a New Spirituality
Chiara Lubich, ISBN: 978-1-56548-432-0

Tending the Mustard Seed: Living the Faith in Today's World
Dennis J. Billy, C.Ss.R., ISBN: 978-1-56548-475-7

Focolare: Living a Spirituality of Unity in the United States
Thomas Masters & Amy Uelmen, ISBN: 978-1-56548- 374-3

The Cry of Jesus Crucified and Forsaken
Chiara Lubich, ISBN 978-1-56548-159-6

The Art of Loving
Chiara Lubich, ISBN 978- 1-56548-335-4

A New Way
Chiara Lubich, ISBN 978-1-56548-236-4

 Scan to
join our
mailing list for
discounts and promotions

Periodicals
Living City Magazine, www.livingcitymagazine.org

On line Resources
http://www.focolare.org/en - this site enables you to read current
experiences of putting the gospel into action.